COMING OUT SOLO

A Memoir

RITUPARNA ROY

Clever Fox® PUBLISHING

Chennai • Bangalore

CLEVER FOX PUBLISHING
Chennai, India

Published by CLEVER FOX PUBLISHING 2025

ISBN: 978-93-6707-716-0

Dedication

To Baba, once again… for being my Banyan.

&

To Didi, for being there.

CONTENTS

ACKNOWLEDGEMENTS

This book grew out of a blog, KOLKATA DIARIES (KD), which I wrote primarily from the end of 2018 to 2022. My first and deepest thanks are to its readers, over four years and more. They are too numerous to be mentioned individually; I remain grateful to each one of them.

In January 2020, when my maiden collection of shorts – *Gariahat Junction* – turned two, I had written an appreciation post (as part of KD) where I specifically acknowledged those who have been generally encouraging of my writing during that time (see p.232). Most of them remain so. In July 2023, I reached out to a few of my most regular/engaged readers about the idea of a book based on the blog. I cherish the responses I received from them – Paromita Mukherjee, Manjima Chatterjee, Brototi Dasgupta, Nandini Bhattacharya, Sudeshna Chakraborti, Uma Biswas and Anasuya Bhar– because that is what gave me the confidence to seek representation for *Coming Out Solo*.

There are, however, a few who have played a special part in the genesis of this book – Saikat Majumdar and Anurima Chanda, foremost among them. Saikat was the first one with whom I discussed the possibility of this book when KD was still young. And we continued that conversation, off and on, for several years. He was always honest with his feedback.

Anurima's enthusiasm for this work – ever since our short stint as colleagues in a private undergraduate college – has been boundless, and her empathy with the struggle I faced in trying to overcome self-censorship in my writing, a gift during a transitional phase of KD.

Pinaki De was prescient in foreseeing how KD would eventually evolve out of that transition when I spoke to him about it, in passing, while discussing another book that still remains shelved.

Barnita Bagchi enthused me by reminding - as only a feminist scholar can - of the long and rich literary tradition of life writing by women.

Between late 2022 and 2024, I was agonizingly divided between two books – between seeking representation for this memoir and writing a book on Partition art, in and from Bengal. It is Vishnupriya Sengupta who impressed upon me the necessity and importance of pursuing the publication of the memoir with a force of conviction that left no room for procrastination.

In the phase of my long dithering, Reema Ahmad was most understanding. I had reached out to her in connection with a publishing contact, but the WhatsApp texts soon became long ruminations and voice notes on vacillation, which she patiently heard out and responded to by sharing her own experience of the same. Bhaswati Ghosh played a similar role, two years later, in exchanging notes about the writing life, and the centrality of waiting in it. Finally, Maitreyee Bhattacharjee Chowdhury told me just the things I wanted to hear at the time I needed to hear them.

I thank them all, from the bottom of my heart – individually and collectively – for giving me strength and clarity when I lacked them. If I have missed anyone, I humbly ask their pardon!

I would also like to thank the team at Clever Fox – especially Kani, Suriya and Shweta – for making this book possible, and especially for trying to honour the publication date I had requested for.

I have dedicated this book to my father (Prof. Birendra Narayan Roy) and my elder sister (Nilanjana Ray) – to whom I have remained precious, lifelong. And I have chosen my daughter Srishti's gift of a portrait on my 50th (when she was herself 11) as the cover art, as I find it the most apposite, given the role she had played as my partner in the journey that I have shared here.

PREFACE

I returned to Kolkata in 2017 after a decade of living and working in the Netherlands. It was not just a relocation back to a hometown, but the beginning of a radical new phase in my life: returning home with a small child to live with my recently widowed father, leaving behind a marriage of eighteen years. It also meant starting over in my career from scratch, at 43. My octogenarian father was devastated, but he stood by me.

When I returned in 2017, I was very invested in writing: after two academic books, I had written a collection of short stories for which I was seeking representation and I was one-third into an epistolary novel. But my writing had to take a back seat while I tried to settle my daughter down to a completely new life and looked for a stable teaching position within the city, even as I initiated a dream project of establishing a Partition Museum in Kolkata. Things became even more challenging when my father fell severely ill and never quite recovered. There was simply no scope for any kind of substantial writing in such a scenario, but I felt I would die if I could not write at least *something*. Hence, I decided to start a blog: KOLKATA DIARIES (henceforth, KD). I had been blogging for a while by then, first on Indian Cinema (read Hindi and Bengali films) and then on my life in the Netherlands. I had taken well to the genre and was motivated to continue when I found an engaged readership on Facebook.

My first post in KD was in February 2018, but there was a long gap after that, and it was only from the end of that year that I started writing regularly, and continued doing so for the next four years.

✦✦✦

Looking back, I find KD can be divided into three distinct phases: the first year – end 2018 to 2019; the pandemic years – 2020 and 2021; and the year life returned to normalcy – 2022. These three phases constitute the three main sections of my memoir.

I. Coming Back Home (end 2018–2019)

The initial intention was only to archive the various facets of my renewed relationship with the city of Kolkata, as it bore out in my personal and professional life. People were as important to it as the place – not just the father and the child I lived with, but those whose lives impinged upon ours.

My present was, however, inextricably intertwined with my past in Kolkata. I was living in a home I had grown up in, and sharing everything in it with a child that I had previously shared with an elder sister. And there was the perpetual absent presence of my mother, whose memory defined my life in many ways. My childhood, adolescent, and young adult past in Kolkata thus often surfaced in KD, even as I wrote about my new present.

II. Coping with Covid (2020–2021)

During the pandemic, KD was naturally taken up with it, with the enormous challenges of the confined life – for both my daughter and me. Though we did not lose any immediate family member to the virus, my life changed irrevocably after my father was institutionalized in a dementia care home and I left my teaching job in a private undergraduate college.

III. Coming Out Solo (2022)

Till then, I had focused on the external trappings of my life, judiciously avoiding the elephant in the room. It took me four years to spell out my single status. That courage came only after my divorce. I "came out" in 2022, in a series of hard-hitting, brutally honest posts that I had refrained from writing earlier, in which I dealt with several dirty D's – divorce, dementia, and depression; also, the deplorable state of higher education in my city, which adversely affected the second phase of my career in it. I chose significant dates in the calendar to bust myths about their regular connotations, at least in my life: 'Mother's Day', 'Father's Day', 'Teacher's Day', 'Bijoya Dashami' and 'Diwali'.

The KD years have thus been years of evolution of the self and a re-fashioning of identity for me.

Prologue And Epilogue

I lost my mother suddenly to a cerebral stroke in August 2016. It took me six months to articulate my grief to myself – on the occasion of my first Birthday without her. The 'Prologue' of this book is that articulation. Soon after, in 2017, I would decide to leave my marriage and return to Kolkata from Amsterdam. I was exceptionally close to my mother: her death is a loss I will never live down, but it is also true that it liberated me! Because, with her gone, I could finally make the choice which she would never have accepted. KD explored the lived reality of that choice, as it unfolded from 2018 onwards. The 'Epilogue' of the book is something I am still experiencing…

✦✦✦

A possible book based on the blog had been on my mind since 2019, after a year of sustained interest from my readers. During the pandemic years, it grew substantially, but it was in 2022 that I thought more seriously about it when, to my surprise, my coming-out posts received empathetic, enthusiastic responses. I was frequently told I articulated issues and emotions that many faced or felt but chose not to express, but which were important to address. I was also appreciated for writing with clarity and a sense of fairness about things that are difficult to be rational about, and without blaming anyone. More than anything else, I was praised for my courage to tell my tale.

In mid-2023, I reached out to a cross-section of my most devoted readers over the years, asking their opinion about the idea of the memoir, and they all gave me a resounding thumbs up! My final confidence to set out on the path of publication for the book came from there.

PROLOGUE (2016–2017)

A GRIEF OBSERVED (3 March 2017)

August 2016 marks a watershed in my life. My primordial bond was snapped that month. For as long as I live, I know, I will divide my life into two phases – with and without Ma, before and after August 2016.

15 August 2016: the last conversation

It is India's Independence Day – the 69th. But it is also the day India got partitioned. As a partition scholar, it is the latter that I remember more. I invariably feel sad every year on this day, but today it is mixed with a selfish happiness: two of my articles have been published – one on Ritwik Ghatak in Scroll.in, and another on Holocaust Memorials in Berlin in the Wire.in. I am particularly thrilled about the latter, as it is based on a recent research trip of mine to Berlin to study something close to my heart, and marks the beginning of something more substantial that I want to do.

I had already sent Baba-Ma the links to my articles, and I called them in the afternoon to get their feedback. There is a whole ritual to this: whenever I write a new piece, I send the final draft to my parents; I call them to say I have sent it; Baba then goes rushing to the nearest internet café and brings home a printout. Ma reads it first – and then many times more – before Baba does. She had once told me how she read: "Prothome gograshe gili, tarpor tariye tariye pori" (I gulp it down the first time – and then savour it, in the subsequent reads). She is a diligent reader: she underlines passages she likes, clarifies points she is not satisfied with, critiques what she feels is missing or not good enough. I expect her to read my piece the moment she gets it in her hand – no matter which time of the day it is, how her health is, or whether she has finished with the day's work or not. She is my oldest, most loyal reader – and I am shameless in my demands upon her. She obliges willingly, happily, every time. This time, too!

She tells me she was moved by reading my Berlin piece and came to know a lot of new things in it. We have a long conversation about it, during which she informs me that she has actually read the article directly online. This is a first! I congratulate her on her evolution as a reader and we have a good laugh over it! But her voice sounds tired. She complains of a headache… and then brushing it aside… tells me for the zillionth time that she has faith in my writing; and though she may not live to see it, she *knows* that one day I will make it as a writer.

I am always grateful for her abiding faith in me, but I get mad whenever she adds that bit… that she may not live to see my success as a writer. I argue with her, "Why not?" But today, I am in a good mood. So, I let that pass. I tell her, instead, with barely suppressed excitement, how well the year has gone for me. Teaching in the spring semester had been very hectic, but fulfilling. And I also managed to write quite a bit during that time – new blog posts for my website, several articles for e-zines. Other good things had happened – the principal being, S getting admitted to the international school we wanted her to. And then July turned out to be such a glorious month for me! My bosom pal came visiting, and we got to spend exclusive time together after eons; soon after, we went for a family holiday in Rome;

and then I went to Berlin. All of that in the same month… it was too good for me. Too good to be true! I tell Ma I have never had a happier month in all my 10 years in the Netherlands. She says (like mothers invariably do), "Don't talk like that about your luck". Then she kisses me and keeps down the phone.

17 August 2016: all over, in a snap

I get a call from Baba around 8 pm. Ma has had a sudden, severe cerebral stroke. Both my sister (who lives in New Jersey) and I rush to Kolkata… but it is too late. By the time we reach the 19th morning, she is already in coma… and then within a day, she passes away. The next three weeks are a blur…

*****

In search of metaphors

What do you do when the dearest person in your life is snatched away from you without warning? You are in trauma. You grieve. You try to come to terms with the loss. But 'trauma', 'grief', 'loss' are all words that fall short of the actual experience. For six months now, words have failed me… I do not know how to articulate my grief… hence, I have been looking for metaphors to do the job for me. By making figurative comparisons/drawing parallels, I can perhaps try and convey my state to others, I can perhaps myself fathom the enormity of my loss…

September 2016

We have just returned to Amsterdam, after Ma's 'sraddha'. S joins her Kindergarten the next day. She has already missed her very first week of school (she and her dad had joined me in Kolkata just a day after I had reached there). It is a completely new school routine for her and me… and, thankfully, I get totally engrossed in it. I had had no time to mourn in the three weeks in Kolkata… there was too much to do. I need time to myself. I cannot socialize, but I do meet people while dropping and picking up S from school. And every time I do, I have a surreal experience. Everybody seems to speak to me from far away as if a vast distance separates us and their voice is being carried over to me in faint echoes. I think I am losing my mind…

It is something else: I have a tremendous sense of dislocation. Ma was my anchor in the world; with her gone, I have lost my sense of mooring. People talk about the ground beneath their feet being taken away after a shocking or traumatic event. For me, it is different – I am dislocated…

I feel I belong to a different planet.

October 2016

S and I are playing hide and seek, her favourite game at home. I know where she will hide, for the most part. But at times she does surprise me by hiding in peculiar niches in our huge apartment. I decide to surprise her when my turn comes for the third time. I hide behind our couch in the living room. It is a large L-shaped couch, placed against the wall on one side and windows on the other. But it does not touch the wall. There is a gap of about fifteen inches all around, so that you can just about walk around it to open windows, draw the blinds, etc. S frequently hides there, as she can be completely hidden from view, and usually crouches somewhere in the middle, so that you have to walk through the narrow passage some distance to get to her. I decide to try this myself. I assume since this spot is her favourite, she would automatically come to search for me here. But she does not quite expect me to squeeze in and crouch down behind the sofa like she does. She comes from the other end of the apartment and goes about her search systematically, room by room – starting from the master bedroom where she is, followed by the guest bedroom, the study, the bathrooms, the kitchen and then the living room. Coming here, she first looks for me behind the door, where there is ample space to hide. When she starts out at the guest bedroom, she has a chirpy, mischief-ridden voice, all braced for fun … waiting to do the 'bhoo' which she loves, and which is the entire point of the exercise – the 'bhoo', and her cackling laughter afterwards. But by the time she reaches the living room, her voice has changed: "Mamma, where are you?" is no more sing-song. It has a trace of fear. She looks around tentatively, goes out of the room, and then comes back again. "Mamma, mamma", she calls out urgently. And then there is silence for a while. I think she must be stealthily coming behind me in the narrow passage to catch me from behind as I do with her. I look back. But no, she is not there. Suddenly, I hear her cry. I immediately stand up… and see her sitting on the sofa, face covered with both her palms, crying to herself. I rush to her. "What happened, baby? Why are you crying?" She removes her palms from her tear-stricken face and mutters, "Because...because... I can't find you", and then, letting out a loud sob, flings her arms around my neck. I take her on my lap, hold her tight. I cannot restrain my own tears. Usually, whenever I need to comfort her, I say, "I am here, shona". But at that moment, I say: "I too can't find my mamma, beta". She does not hear it. She is still crying. We cling to each other.

I am S. I cannot find my Mamma. I feel lost without her.

November 2016

It is a rainy, windy day, after a storm the night before. Winter is here. The leaves have all fallen. The day is exceptionally bleak and dark, wet and chilly, with more storm clouds gathering. There is not even a hint of the sun. It is a desolate landscape, with the bare branches of the trees looking forlorn in the unrelieving grey of the sky that envelops it. That is how I feel within me. Desolate. Three months after losing Ma, I have found the perfect metaphor to describe my state.

I am a desolate winter landscape, enveloped in grey.

December 2016

It's my first time going to Kolkata without Ma. To home, without the one who embodied it.

January 2017

We go to see *Dangal* — Baba, Didi and I, along with S. We are all Aamir Khan fans, and it is also so appropriate: a dad and his two daughters going to see a story about a dad and his two daughters!

Last year, we saw *Bajirao Mastani*. That would be our last film together as a family. Had Ma lived, she would have loved *Dangal*. And would have cried a lot, I know. But, to my surprise, Baba is also crying, sitting beside me, at all the critical moments of the film. Everyone knows it is based on the true story of Haryanvi wrestler Mahavir Singh Phogat, and how he achieved the impossible dream of making wrestlers out of his daughters, Geeta and Babita Singh Phogat. The film presents a far more dramatic version of events. One of the high points in the second part is the clash between Geeta's official coach and her father about the way she should play her game. Her coach asks her to be defensive, while her father, who has been her principal trainer since her early teenage years, knows that attack is her natural style, and advises her to play her game her way. The last half hour is full of action-packed wrestling sequences, the actor playing Geeta doing it so convincingly that you forget it is a film. In every one of her major fights at the end, the film shows Geeta's father in the audience – cheering her on, giving pep talks during the breaks, sitting stolidly observing every move of hers so that he can give her constructive feedback after the game. In the final scene of the film, where Geeta is about to create history – by becoming the first Indian female wrestler ever to win a gold medal in a major championship – the father unfortunately cannot sit in the audience. He does arrive in the stadium but is forcibly kept away from the game. All through that game, Geeta looks back to where her sister is sitting and where her father should have been – but he is absent. She keeps hoping she will see him and gets steadily disappointed when he fails to arrive. And then, in the penultimate phase of the game, she finally braces herself after she remembers what her father had once told her: that though he has taught her all he could, the actual fight will always be hers. Watching that scene, I am crying inconsolably in the dark theatre…

I realize I am Geeta Singh Phogat, fighting alone in the arena of life, with my biggest cheerleader gone forever.

✦✦✦

I am an alien belonging to a different planet;

I am a little girl feeling lost without her Mamma;

I am a desolate landscape enveloped in grey;

I am a wrestler fighting ever stronger opponents, with my coach and chief cheerleader gone.

In the coming months and years, I will add metaphor upon metaphor… yet nothing will ever approximate, will come even close to conveying the hole in my life…

COMING BACK HOME (END 2018–2019)

BACK TO PRESIDENCY (4 February 2018)

I started teaching as a Guest Faculty in the English Department of Presidency University a day after I relocated back to Kolkata last summer. In the initial weeks, I was racked with nostalgia on the one hand, remembering my student life 25 years back; and on the other, trying to absorb all the changes that the institution has undergone in its new avatar as an autonomous university (from an erstwhile undergraduate college affiliated to Calcutta University).

There is much that is new in the main building (where the English Department is housed): the 'stairway to heaven' is now wrought in marble, heaven itself can be alternately accessed by an elevator, the classrooms have shrunk in size, the students have doubled in number, the Seminar Library is now the HOD's office, the PCR is virtually unrecognizable, a disproportionate installation gobbles up the quadrangle, the steps on the portico have vanished, as have the 'khops' in the corridors of the ground floor – all of them levelled out.

There are more: the ground-floor corridor leading up to the main Arts Library now holds temporary exhibitions on its walls, and there are new staff offices and a sizable new auditorium en route to the canteen (on which I cannot comment, as I have hardly been there). The most striking new feature, however, is the names of innumerable eminent alumni of the erstwhile college chiselled out on the walls on all floors — an ever-present reminder of the excellence and range of achievements that this pioneering institution has stood for, for 200 years: a legacy that needs to be upheld.

Some features of the building, thankfully, have remained the same: the high ceilings and the long, wide corridors on every floor, which continue to give a sense of expansive space that is always a welcome relief after negotiating the congestion of College Street on the way to the University.

This is the best place I could start my second innings of teaching in Kolkata. I feel at home here in a way I do not anywhere else in the city, even when it does not harbour a single familiar face from my time. Even after all the structural changes I have enumerated above.

There are other changes, too, which have to do with me personally: what I am teaching here is vastly different from what I was doing the last couple of years at LIAS, Leiden and LUC, the Hague. The English Department offers a very interesting and holistic syllabus spread over the five years of BA and MA, out of which my assignments primarily include English canonical texts. I am also having to acquaint myself with all the new UGC rules and regulations over the last decade: in short, trying to get back into the shoes of being an Indian academic in India.

What has helped me adjust to the changes (and it is still very much a work-in-progress) is the attitude of my colleagues – ever friendly and helpful – within the Department, the immense goodwill and moral support of my friends and former colleagues in the city, and the continuing encouragement of my former teachers. I am thankful to them all.

I like being part of the English Faculty at Presidency: a young, dynamic bunch of people who bring a range of expertise to bear upon the courses being taught. And it is of course ultimately the students – bright, attentive, and engaged (for the most part) – who make the teaching worthwhile for me.

It is a rare privilege to be able to serve the institution that has been a shaping influence in one's life. I am enjoying that privilege while it lasts…!

PS:

One very important fact about the English Department at Presidency: like any department in any given university, it faces its own set of challenges – but 'vacant seats' is not one of them. If anything, here the problem is just the opposite – it could do with more classrooms and more teaching staff!

BACK FROM THE JAWS OF DEATH (18 March 2018)

Today, after five weeks, Sunday was a day of rest. Since 10th February, we have been through a nightmare with my father's health. We initially admitted him into a nursing home, but after twelve days there, we shifted him to a private hospital. Except for the last week, he was almost entirely in the ICU – fighting a peculiar instance of 'acute kidney injury' whose exact cause could not be fathomed even by specialists, after all relevant investigations. I do not want to go into the details of the protracted treatment, the many complications that it led to in a frail 82-year-old body, the dead ends we faced several times over five harrowing weeks, and the appalling lack of professionalism we witnessed in some medical establishments.

The physical/ practical/logistical aspects of this crisis were, of course, demanding. But it was the emotional roller-coaster that was the hardest to cope with: from shock (we had no idea that Baba had a kidney problem) to gripping fear (of losing him so soon after Ma) to being almost stoically prepared for the inevitable, to a sense of immense relief and gratefulness that he has been granted a new lease of life, and now, finally, trying to accept the considerably reduced autonomy of his body.

Baba is back. That is all that matters... I have been telling myself these last three days. Though I must admit, it is hard to reconcile the fragile old patient who has come back home, worlds away, as he is from the self-sufficient, proud man I know. Who, till a while back, defied every stereotype of old age that one can think of.

INDIANA (28 October 2018)

Tucked away in Shyama Charan De Street – one of the innumerable by lanes of College Street – it is easy to miss INDIANA if you are not a regular visitor. But if you happen to be a student or teacher in the College Street 'para', or have anything to do with the (still) flourishing book-trade there, you would know Amit da and *meshomoshai* (his father). In fact, chances are you would be referred to them by other book shops when you cannot find this or that book. I did not use 'this or that' dismissively – I meant it as a compliment for the eclectic collection that INDIANA has always housed ever since I first chanced upon it in the late 90s.

I had just cleared NET-JRF then and had decided to work on Partition fiction in English, having specialized in Indian-English literature in my Master's. There were not many secondary texts available (or even written) in my research area, then. And the bookshops that normally catered to 'English Literature' could not help me much. Libraries in Kolkata had the same problem. In such a scenario, Amit da came as a saviour. He routinely got me books that I could not get anywhere else in that pre-Amazon era. And he regularly couriered them to me in the many places that I happened to live, for short or long periods, and for altogether unpredictable reasons, while doing my doctoral and postdoctoral research – Bangalore, Chennai, Amstelveen, Amsterdam, Stuttgart. In fact, those couriers have been the one constant in my accidentally peripatetic life of the last two decades. And the INDIANA label also graces the dust jacket of half the collection of books in my personal library – my only material possession in life!

I had befriended Amit da first, and his father later. And strangely enough, in my years away from Kolkata, another association developed: with my parents, this time, when they were trying to publish my mother's collection of short-shorts (or *anugolpo*) in Bangla – *MUKH MICHHIL* (A procession of faces). For various reasons, things did not work out with the publishers that Amit da had recommended to them and he ended up publishing it himself, though he does not publish Bangla.

This father-son duo is a rare breed – never allowing business realities to tarnish their love of good books and their determination to house the same in their shop. It has been revamped recently, but even in its most chaotic avatar, it was my favourite bookshop in the world. It remains so even after my return.

Thank God, it is still there. The last time that I bought books from INDIANA was yesterday, with S in tow... and so the story continues...!

AMADER BAUL (4 November 2018)

He still comes twice a month – *ektara* in hand, dishevelled hair tied back in a jumbled knot, beard flowing down to his chest, clad in a *gerua* punjabi and dhoti, with a red *gamcha* around his neck, *jhola* on his shoulder, and worn-out sandals on his feet. And he still sings the same songs – the trademark *baul* (wandering minstrels of Bengal) songs of mystic love for an elusive 'moner manush', of life and death, the eternal yearnings of the heart.

But he is a shadow of himself now: his voice has cracked, no more able to sustain the high notes, and after having sung barely two songs, he takes his leave. Physically, too, he has shrunk, with an incredible sadness sculpted on his face.

In his heydays, 25/30 years back, he was a robust man – in body and voice. And usually sang upwards of an hour in full-throated ease. His eyes would mostly be closed, his soul immersed in the beauty of the music and the profundity of the thoughts contained in the lyrics. And there would be a faint smile hovering on his lips, when, opening his eyes, he found an appreciative audience - more than a dozen pairs of innocent eyes - staring down at him from their balconies. I was one of them.

I grew up in a housing complex where three blocks of flats and their balconies faced each other in a semicircle with a sizable playground in their midst. It is here that he sang, and between songs, would move around the circumference of that circle, and sometimes stand right in the middle of the playground – making it a stage performance without a stage.

The bunch of us kids growing up together in the complex ranged all the way from primary school to college and university. It was, however, the primary school children who constituted the most loyal audience of the baul, and among them, no one heard him with more attention than me. I was actually egged on by my mother, who, in between her household chores, would give me money to give to the baul; and sometimes, pausing in her work, would listen to a song or two, herself. "What a voice", she would frequently marvel, and had a great desire to tape-record it in a cassette player. She had gone through this major recording phase – recording the voices and memories of our grandmothers when they visited us, our (my sister and mine) stupid conversations at home, her favourite poems in her own voice; all of them on a PERK tape recorder. Unfortunately, the baul's voice was never recorded, and very few of the other recordings survive as well.

Ironically, the more technologically advanced audio systems became, the less enthusiastic we got about recording in the family. The PERK was followed in our home by a VIDEOCON 'two-in-one' cassette player and recorder, which was succeeded after more than a decade by a PHILIPS radio, cassette-cum-disc player. And then with the coming of computers, we started listening on desktops, later laptops, and finally mobiles.

My mother's enthusiasm for recording had waned long ago. And we never had much time to indulge in such luxuries after school. In our college and university years, we were never there when the baul came to sing. And later, most of us children left the building - for studies, work, or marriage - to other places within India and abroad. With us gone, the baul lost his principal audience. No wonder-eyed girl stood on her balcony to listen to him. The stage itself changed irrevocably – the playground being transformed into an open garage to accommodate the increasing cars in the building. Only some change was thrown down to him, wrapped in paper or plastic from the upper floors, and through balcony railings by those on the ground floor.

"*Tara ma, keu nei*"? (Is there no one?) He cries out these days after singing – more piercingly, desperately, than ever before, trying to tease out a reluctant audience. Some change still comes his way in response to that – usually from a few fixed families who have retained their sympathy for him despite his failing voice. But the honest answer to his question is: "No, there is none".

ALL THAT GLITTERS IS GOLD (and DIAMOND)! (10 November 2018)

What jewellery did you buy this Pujo/ Dhanteras/ Diwali? None? Not even with all the discounts? –"25% off on making charge", "50% off..." on something else. Too bad! Has no husband/ boyfriend/ brother solicitously asked you to download the "ANJALI App" on your mobile so that you can shop for gold online? You are damn unlucky then! For just like everything else, gold is now available at the click of a button, its stores accessible no matter where they may be located geographically. But does available/accessible automatically make it affordable?? That is an irritating question, I know; it spoils all the fun of this endlessly happy festive season of ours.

It is difficult to resist the temptation to be 'happy' (read, 'wear jewellery') when the most radiantly beautiful women urge you to it, wearing the choicest gold, diamond and gems that the best of brands can muster. And they urge you everywhere. Huge billboards of them line up above all the arterial roads of the city. Looking at them, it is difficult to choose between a Kajol in a JOYALLUKAS choker, a Koel Mullick in signature ANJALI pujo-ensembles, or a Kriti Kharbanda in a new-age P.C. CHANDRA dangler.

These billboards are not new. But over the years, they have gone bigger and bolder, rivalling even film posters in their size and grandeur, just as the jewellery they advertise have become heavier and more resplendent. There are many kinds of jewellery on display, of course – bridal collections being the most common/ popular among them, followed closely by Pujo and Diwali collections.

Who buys that jewellery, I wonder? Who wears them? And where? Apart from the Red-Carpet appearances of Superstars in Film Festivals (caps intended) and the weddings/celebrations of the super-rich, I cannot think of anyone wearing those necklaces, bracelets, earrings... all of which, from the looks of it, must feel heavy on the body as it undoubtedly does on the purse!

Going by the billboards, one would think Indian women have nothing else to do but buy and wear jewellery. Wait. Wear, not buy. In all the ads, it is usually the parents or the husband who buys them that. You have this feeling that while women choose their own cosmetics, jewellery is given to them. That is actually true, at least in my experience. I know very few women who can afford to buy jewellery for themselves. Especially of the kind that is endorsed up there, whichever way one's head turns – when on a normal, harried day one is commuting to work, or picking/dropping off one's child at school.

It was not always like this, though. Back in the late-1990s and early post-millennial years, I liked TANISHQ when it came up with the idea of wearable, affordable jewellery, targeted especially for the working woman – dainty stuff that one could wear to the office, or slightly more elaborate ones that one could choose to deck oneself with while partying or socializing in the evenings. They still have a line of light jewellery - MIA. But you do not see that line on billboards. You only see what Rani Padmavati wore in Rajasthan seven centuries ago, or else, what her screen impersonation can afford to wear on Diwali.

Every city has a gold 'patti' – where you have many small shops trading in gold and jewels for generations, clustered together in one neighbourhood. So does Kolkata, the one in Bowbazar in central Calcutta, being one of the oldest and most famous of them all. (My wedding set from my parents was bought from there). But there are others, too. When I started teaching full-time in an undergraduate college in South Kolkata way back in 2001, I daily walked past one such cluster in and around Ekdalia on my way back from work. They did not need to advertise themselves. People came to buy gold from them anyway, all through the year. But there was a perceptible change a couple of years down the line, when I started noticing small rectangular plaques advertising a well-known Bengali jeweller on the railings of dividers on Rashbehari Avenue. The big posters were then still mostly of films and occasionally of products of foreign cosmetic brands – a L'OREAL lipstick or a MAYBELLINE eyeliner. And then a whole new trend began, just around the time I left the country in 2007: more and more names of jewellery shops/brands - some of which I had never heard before - started surfacing on billboards. And it was not just top-notch actresses who endorsed them, but also new and upcoming models.

I confess I am in a time warp. Though I visited Kolkata almost every year in the decade that I was away, and had seen the phenomenon of jewellery obsession unfolding, I find it difficult to gulp in that nonsense now that I am living here. I yearn for the boring gold-patti days when gold was bought and sold without fanfare, and I really wish jewellery had not been blown out of proportion in our skyline. Since it is so far away from the reality of the lives led by most women in India – whether single or married, homemakers or working wives/mothers. And especially given the fact that good jobs are so few and daily living is pretty expensive (even in a cheap city like Kolkata). Who buys all that glitter? I wonder every day, confronted with ever-new advertisements, as I go to work at a new University. No academic for sure. In a system where even Ph.D. holders can get as abysmally paid as Rs. 300/ per lecture as Guest Faculty, jewellery is a distant dream. Even with the discounts.

'MESHOMOSHAI' and HIS NEW NIECES (17 November 2018)

My widowed father's new household is filled with abandoned women (incidentally, all migrants from Bangladesh and all residing in Dattapukur). They numbered three at one point. Now there are two. One cooks, the other cleans, and both double up as night nurses at different places.

They could never have been here if my mother was alive. She never allowed any cook for all the 44 years of her married life; and though she was certainly open to domestic help, when the local ones could not be relied on, she downright refused to hire 'from the Centre' because of their high hourly rates. Even with a daughter earning in dollars and dying to contribute and make them live comfortably, Ma resolutely stuck to the lifestyle that a pensioner's wife could afford.

After Ma passed away in August 2016, Dipti and Soma (names changed) entered Baba's life - ostensibly to take care of him and his empty home, but also ended up partially filling the void in it by making him their 'meshomoshai' (uncle - maternal aunt's husband). Ever since, as with everyone else who comes within his orbit, he has been full of unsolicited advice for their health and wellbeing ("Drink a cup of Women's Horlicks every morning") and the future of their sons ("Why is your son not enrolling for college? Ask him to contact me… I want to talk to him"). They partly indulge this incorrigible 'teacher' in him who simply can't 'retire', partly (privately) scoff at him. They are also clearly irritated by his fussiness about vegetables (which he does not allow to be cooked if they do not have the right look/size/colour/

texture), and his all-new obsession with cleanliness (a small fortune is spent every month on Nimyl and Dettol, with some variety of the latter gracing the house at every point that there is a basin - bathroom, kitchen, back balcony - so that he can wash his hands wherever he is for any number of insane reasons). But they were the ones who were most distraught when he was in the ICU of a private hospital for four weeks earlier in the year with a kidney problem.

Baba's habitual compassion for the needy and the poor is a tad bit extra for them. It stems from the fact that they are abandoned single mothers. They had briefly - at different times - shared the story of their struggle with him, and later, in more detail with my sister and me.

Their trajectory as poor working women is not a unique one, but inspiring nevertheless: for Dipti, it involved leaving a child on the other side of the border with her parents for a long time; for Soma, it was having to frequently go without food for days and bear the responsibility and pain of not being able to allay her children's hunger; for both, providing the child (Dipti)/children (Soma) a rudimentary education while doing violently exploitative and contingent work for years. But theirs is also an enabling journey – from abysmal pays to good rates, from sheer penury to being financially solvent, from living in the stinky corridor of a distant relative's house to a spacious rented room of one's own with a proper designated area for a kitchen and a separate bath, from being inexperienced and shy/afraid/anxious/young women to emerging as self-confident and self-sufficient individuals.

Hearing their stories, I have realized that just as love has many hues, so has abandonment. Despite all that she has faced, Dipti retains a tenderness for the husband who had once loved her and nursed her during a major illness. She says she understands why he betrayed her, and then goes on to give an irrational explanation (irrational for me, very rational for her) for it: blaming it all on family intrigue and an oh-so helpless husband marrying again (without the knowledge of his first wife and child) against his choice. Soma has faced the worst kind of physical abuse by her perpetually drunk and irresponsible husband (and eternally absent father of her sons). She is enormously relieved to have got rid of him... which was not at all easy to accomplish, as he kept coming back to claim his rights. Hence, in her case, the term 'abandoned' needs to be qualified: she was abandoned by her husband during their marriage, from which she actively sought to liberate herself. She is enormously and unashamedly happy to be alone, and to return home only to her boys. It is enough for her to love them and live for them.

They both insist on returning home every day to their children, who are now adults – even when being full-time domestic help would have actually helped them earn more and spared them a lot of time and energy. So why did they not do that, I had once asked. "To keep a watchful eye", I was told – youngsters going astray being too common in their milieu.

And so, they commute every day on the Bonga local to get about three precious hours with their sons in the late afternoon. In the evening, they commute against the tide of the floating population of Kolkata. While millions leave the city to return home in far-flung towns and villages, they come to the metropolis to start their working day in the evening as night nurses. They are both always dressed impeccably – sari pinned and pleated to perfection, hair tied up in a bun, and an always bursting handbag on their shoulder. And… vermilion on their hair-parting, *bindi* on their forehead, *sakha-pala* on their wrists. I never asked them why they did that. Baba had told me that part long before I became familiar with them, and I would have guessed anyway. They retain the marital signs of Bengali Hindu women to protect themselves. It is the easiest armour they can carry to shield themselves from unwanted male attention and unwarranted queries on trains during daily commutes.

It makes me wonder about the nature of their liberation and self-sufficiency: years of lonely toil, trauma, and courageous confrontation with fate, only to end up masking it with the external trappings of marriage. It is a daily lie/important survival strategy in their lives that their teacher-'meshomoshai', can do nothing to change.

THE SKY ABOVE US (24 November 2018)

For nine years, we lived in a huge apartment in Amsterdam – five of them with S. It was on the ninth floor of a tall residential building in the district of Buitenveldert in Amsterdam Zuid (South). The beauty of the apartment lay chiefly in the 'view' – with a vast stretch of the Amsterdam skyline visible whenever one looked out from whichever room. And that skyline was defined not just by buildings but also by trees and airplanes. In the immediate vicinity were the heads of long rows of trees that seemed to grow taller every year, their green leaves tender with every renewal in spring and resplendent every summer. And Schiphol being not far away, planes could be seen passing by all through the day: some would go past really near, and look massive; others were far away and small. But of course, above and beyond everything else was the sky itself – that wondrous canopy of nature. It was no small boon for us that no matter what the weather - be it the constant drizzles through the year, the depressing all-permeating grey of the winters, or the glorious sun-drenched days of the summer - the sky was always available and accessible to us.

The biggest room in our home was the master bedroom, the best part of which was its windows: wide glass windows that lined the entire stretch of a wall. Standing in the room, one of course saw the trees and buildings; but lying down on the bed, especially at a particular angle, framed by the windows, all one could see was the sky – huge rectangular blocks of uninterrupted sky. Over the years, lying down and watching that sky became my own definition of 'rest', mostly indulged on Sunday afternoons after lunch, with or without S. And, at times, if I lay still and stared into that vast expanse of the sky long enough, the borders of the window-frame dissolved and I felt as if I was being projected into space. It was the closest to a 'mystic' experience that I have known.

Like all other things that I loved about Amsterdam, I cherish the memory of that sky. So, does S. For months after returning to Kolkata, she would sorely miss Amsterdam. And keep asking me, "Mamma, when will we go back home?" She thought we were on an extended holiday in Kolkata, one of her annual trips stretched too long. She missed all aspects of her 5-year-old life in Amsterdam, particularly our home. And very often, as I tried to put her to sleep on weekend afternoons, she would remember being bundled up with me in bed and looking out at the sky together. A wistful smile would spread across her lips then.... and she would invariably end her recounting with: "It was so beautiful, na?" I agreed, wholeheartedly.

Here we see a different sky. It is not associated with rest, light or space. The sky is a presence in our lives only at night and mostly when the stars are out. We do not see much of it during the day, which simply whizzes past in a furious whirl of activity. We also experience sleep differently: even on the days we are at home, it is no longer a rest in communion with nature, but an anaesthetized oblivion in a cold, dark room with the AC on and all the doors and windows shut. Shut firmly to keep out heat and dust and mosquitoes – heat and dust during the day, mosquitoes from late afternoon to night. This is unavoidable in a tropical climate with the fear of dengue looming large everywhere. But keeping the heat and infections at bay, unfortunately, also entails shutting out the light. Shutting out the sky. Living in self-contained/constrained spaces, with nothing to look out at and only feeling hemmed in.

S is still a small child and highly adaptable. Hence, after the initial trauma of our relocation from Amsterdam to Kolkata, she has coped well with an essentially hemmed-in existence. She has also managed to develop a new association with the sky. She knows that her 'dida' (my late mother) has now become a star, and taking up that lead with enthusiasm, ever so often, she searches for that star in the night sky. On days that she can spot the brightest, she pulls me out on the balcony: "Mamma, see, see, dida". And then she weaves a story about what she thinks her dida is feeling, looking down at us.

I had seen her dida burnt to ashes two years back in front of my eyes. Thinking of her as a star is very difficult after that. I know she lives on in me and my sister in all manner of intangible ways. But I cannot philosophize/intellectualize/romanticize death beyond that. Before Ma's death, I could. After she left, all philosophy falls short of my actual experience of her loss. The searing pain of the first year is gone, but the void remains. As do the silent tears, that still flow unwarranted at odd times for inexplicable reasons.

But I keep my thoughts on death to myself. When S speaks, I indulge the natural storyteller in her. If she has found a way to communicate with a grandmother she has hardly known and can only vaguely remember, who am I to interfere? Besides, her dida would have been delighted with S's imaginative faculty – if she is indeed up there. She had waited very long to see a grandchild. S was her only. But she got to spend only 40 days with S – measured out equally over four trips in four years. Being a star will thus give her access to what she missed out on in real life – S's childhood in Kolkata: seeing her grow, go to school, sing, dance, draw, weave tales, and speak Bangla.

I have thus learnt - gradually, over the last year - to give in to S's belief. That Ma is looking down on us. Hence, on the rare days that I can afford to stand and stare at the night sky, I participate in the relationship that she has forged with a star.

The rectangular block of Amsterdam sky that was mine epitomized rest, feeling one with nature; the cable-streaked semi-circular patch of night sky that I am now re-discovering in Kolkata, with S stands for astral communication with Ma. I have learnt to value both.

KAKIMA (3 January 2019)

When we were growing up, there was no concept of 'play-dates'. There was no necessity. A child had ample playmates in her daily life – neighbours, cousins, and often schoolmates who lived nearby. One habitually spends time with one's peers without mothers having to synchronize complicated routines and spend money to enable their children to 'have fun' in expensive malls and restaurants. Our 'fun' came free – in playgrounds, terraces, balconies and cozy bedrooms. What also invariably came free was the bonding with our friends' mothers – who, over the years, became both surrogate mothers and friends to us. When we met at each other's homes, we chatted with/in the presence of our mothers almost as much as we conversed by ourselves. It was not customary then to slot adults and children into mutually exclusive rooms with the assumption that their worlds are different and cannot meet. Uncles and aunts were an integral part of the joy of our lives, and sometimes the favourite aunt happened to be one's bestie's mom.

I have had aunts galore in my life – doting aunts all, whom I am very fond of. There are two other aunts whom I have loved dearly since my teenage years – my two closest friends' moms. Our trio is no more a trio: one is lost to us… strangely… even in a world teeming in/with communication. Two of us remain bosom pals – clinging to each other, virtually, across continents. All our mothers loved their daughters' best friends, and each shared a distinct relationship with the girls. They had different trajectories as individuals and wives, but as mothers, they grew old and lonely in exactly the same way, as their daughters left them to seek new lives in other cities, and then countries. Two of the mothers have passed away in quick succession. Only one remains. She is very precious to me – not only because of her unfailing love and concern for me for over three decades, but also because she is the only bridge to an aspect of my girlhood that would otherwise have been lost forever.

Today is her Birthday… I wish her many more happy returns!

MY MATRILINEAL INHERITANCE
(3 March 2019)

One of my most precious possessions I have is a photograph, taken in October 2003, of my mother and dida (my maternal grandmother). They are encircling each other's waists and smiling into the camera. On the right of the photograph is Dida – feisty, resilient, impish; on the left, Ma – selfless, honest, hopelessly romantic.

Dida was a wild village girl, very much like Mrinmoyee in Tagore's story, 'Samapti' – given to romping around, climbing trees and playing pranks on others; and just like Amulya in the story, it was precisely this untamed nature of hers that attracted Dadu to her. He was the eldest son of a Zamindar in Jessore – so she had to naturally mend her ways and slip into the role of a 'boro-bou' (eldest daughter-in-law) after her marriage. It mostly meant, she had told me once, having hardly anything to eat after serving meals to a huge household and mothering a string of little brothers and sisters-in-law, the last of whom (the 19th child) was only a few years older than her first-born. She was fourteen at the time, and already a veteran householder by then; the next decade and a half passed by bearing seven children in quick succession. But her world fell apart when she was suddenly widowed at 28, with her children then aged between 2 and 14. With no formal education of her own and cheated out of her husband's inheritance, she brought up her children, who had to adjust from a life of plenty to that of poverty, with an indomitable will and a fierce pride that left no room for others' pity.

Ma - the eldest daughter - was the man of the house from a very tender age, earning herself an education on the strength of scholarships right from school to university and becoming a lecturer of Bengali Literature soon after. Along with her elder brother (with whom she shared a special bond, which was very Nita-Shankar at its core), her maiden life was devoted to standing by her mother, looking after the well-being of her younger siblings, and turning the fortunes of her family from utter destitution to one of lower middle-class gentility. Things didn't change much after her marriage either – as her marital life was completely given over to the new family she created, to supporting her husband's multiple idealistic obsessions, and to her two daughters, whom she chose to bring up, giving up her career.

Ma and Dida were both creative souls. Dida's creativity took myriad forms: in addition to what grandmas of our generation habitually did, like making pickles and sweets ('aachar', 'aamshotto', 'narkel nadu'), she loved gardening. Her home was surrounded by mango and jackfruit trees, and she grew chilies, brinjal and tomato in her own small patchwork garden, tending to them with loving care. Above all, she was a great 'kantha' artist. She wove dozens of them for her ever-increasing family – her seven children and their spouses, fourteen grandchildren and some of their spouses, great grandchildren (she lived to see four of them); her extended relations and their brood.

She also made two in advance for my child-to-be, whom she was desperate to see but who came into the world two years after she was gone. My daughter, S, now uses the gift that Dida had left her. Every time I tuck her in, in her *kantha*, I remember Dida, and marvel at the fact that she is wrapped in the warmth of the love of a great grandmother she has never seen.

There was another unique side to Dida: she wrote poetry. It was somewhat raw but touching, the most memorable ones being those she wrote after she lost her only grandson – a sprightly creature of four, the darling of the family, who died of a sudden heart attack. Dida never lived that loss down.

Ma was immensely talented: a trained Rabindrasangeet singer, an untrained elocutionist, and a closet writer. Poetry was her first love: she read poetry and wrote her own incessantly. But she also wrote fiction, which she never bothered to publish. Her only published work (apart from a book of rhymes for children), a collection of short shorts, came out in 2014, just two years before she passed away. Initially inspired by Banaphool's 'Natun Golpo' and written over a period of time, it is an accomplished work. Unfortunately, it has been able to reach only a limited audience.

Ma's creativity manifested itself in something else, too – her 'sansar'. Domesticity and its inevitable drudgery never bogged her down. Though it took her away from leading a fuller intellectual life, which her teaching career would have given her, she nevertheless turned homemaking into an everyday art that she practiced with thrift and ingenuity till her last years.

Though they had obviously different life trajectories, Ma and Dida were bound intimately by the pain of a primal loss – the sudden, shocking death of Dadu when he was only 42. He was a rare man for his times: a husband who had given both love and respect to a semi-literate wife fourteen years his junior; and a father who, instead of being a stern disciplinarian, doted on his children, none more than his eldest daughter. Ma was only seven when she lost him, but she mourned him all her life. And her life would undoubtedly have been far less thorny had he been around. For Dida, the memory of her husband's love was the only weapon in her widowed armour – that gave her the strength not only to fend off unwarranted male advances, but more importantly, to cope with insurmountable odds.

Pain and loss need to be endured. And they did. But they always wore the badge of endurance with dignity, continually found joy in the little things of life, and sustained themselves with writing.

This is my matrilineal inheritance. I would like to bequeath it to S – hopefully, with a greater quotient of happiness and freedom.

THE NEW FOTOLAB (8 March 2019)

They are a perfect pair. They complement each other and are a study in contrast: she flaunts her white hair, he dyes it black; she means business at all hours, he loves to chat with his customers; she laughs spontaneously and loudly, he is all languid smile and twinkling eyes; she wears bright kurtis, he is clad in sober shirts.

Sakhisona mashi and Swapan mesho. I have known them for almost 40 years now. Mashi was a younger colleague of my mother in a Montessori school named 'East Point' in our neighbourhood, way back in the late 1970s. That was a short phase in my mother's life (some years after she had left her permanent lecturer's job in Bengali Literature in a distant college), but she bonded with many women there. Some yellowing photographs of a long-ago picnic bear testimony to that time. Of the several young women from the school who frequented our home, there were two whom I liked the most – Sakhi mashi and Sraboni mashi. Sraboni mashi visited us the most – always full of gifts and joyful chatter. She was lost to us soon after, however, but Sakhi mashi remained a part of our lives.

Sakhi mashi was a stunner: glowing fair skin, bob-hair, beautiful face, contagious smile. Coupled with a distinctly un-feminine voice! My earliest memory of her is of a vision in white – mashi in a sleeveless white top and black skirt, with skin-leggings, camera hanging from her neck. She illuminated the room with her sheer presence. I had never seen any Bengali woman of my acquaintance dress like that. Or look like that. I was immediately smitten. Another source of attraction was the Nazia and Zoheb Hasan records that she played in her home on Sundays. The small, rented ground-floor apartment in a two-storey house that she and her husband lived in, faced one part of our housing complex – such that I could talk to her across our apartment's small balcony. I would often go over to their place, and once stayed the whole day till a party in the evening (for her anniversary, I think) got over.

I remember being told she had been to Japan. Which was a surprise. I had heard people going to the US and the UK, but I had never heard of anyone going to Japan. That made her even more exotic to me. That aura was only lost when I first visited her on a Sunday and saw her dressed in a nighty, dusting her bedroom with a quick, casual efficiency while humming 'Disco Deewane'.

That efficiency is what she has always brought to her work at THE NEW FOTOLAB as well. If you are ever in Kankurgchi, you cannot miss it. From the crossing, if you are going towards Bengal Chemical, the shop will be to your right. That is the place where it has always been ever since 1978 – when Swapan mesho set it up, even as he worked reluctantly as a Reserve Bank employee.

I admire couples like mashi and mesho who share a common passion. In their case, however, it is not just something that they indulge in only on holidays or on vacations when they let their hair down. It is also their profession, their bread and butter.

Their profession - and professionalism - has benefited all of us locals. For no matter where one lives, all will agree, it is always great to have a photo studio near one which can deftly cater to all manner of emergencies, personal/professional/medical. I have always gone there with urgent needs. I cannot remember doing anything that was not urgent. I also cannot remember anything in my life that FOTOLAB has not been a part of: from the Exams in my student days to job applications in my career (for all of which I needed passport photos), from my wedding to my mother's funeral.

The last time I met them together, true to their personalities – Sakhi mashi got my photos done while carrying on a conversation with me and looking at other customers as well, while mesho tried to bribe me for a longer adda with tea and samosa. "Ektu bosh na" (Do sit for a while), he entreated. I had no time. I never do. He was mock-hurt. "Next time", I promised. Let's see when I can keep it.

✦✦✦

There. That was it. My intended post. In 730 words flat. After writing it (in late December 2018), I went to talk to mashi (early in January 2019). I had written things entirely from memory and went to just cross-check certain facts that I was not entirely sure of before I posted the piece. I, however, came away with not just fact-checks, but a totally different perspective. In the 45 minutes of our conversation unfolded a life that I had never known in all the 40 years of our acquaintance.

First, the fact-check: my very first memory of her turned out to be incorrect. The camera could not have hung from her neck, mashi told me, when I first saw her as a young single woman teaching in 'East Point' – because she came to photography a little later in life, after her marriage. And it was never - and is still not, she emphasized - her passion. It was/is "just work". That was news!

She never had any passion as such, she told me, just a zest for work. Her life was actually defined by her father's early death when she was in high school. With a Bachelor's degree in Economics from Bethune College, she could have easily continued with her studies, but did not – because she needed to earn. And she was very practical and pragmatic in her approach as to how to do it: she embraced new opportunities that came her way, worked hard, and made the best of them before moving on to the next. So that in three short years, she had quite a varied experience. Starting with 'East Point', where she worked part-time, she quickly moved on to a better-paying Kindergarten ('National').

While there, she did a Secretarial course in the afternoons from 'Martin & Burns' which landed her a job at 'Johnson & Johnson' soon after. She had actually not completed the secretarial course, but she had learnt the basics well – had good speed for both typing and shorthand; and being fluent in English and confident in personality, she did well in the GD as well. So, the job was hers. There was also another she had applied for – a desk job at Air India, but she was already married by then. And AI did not want married women on their rolls because of the odd working hours that were involved.

As mashi recounted her early years, the prevailing prejudices against the working women of her generation in the corporate sector became clear: 'Anglos' and 'non-Bengalis' were preferred for secretarial positions, single women for airlines. While she did not make much of these prejudices, she was soon to confront a major one when she started working in THE NEW FOTOLAB. Everybody objected to her "sitting" in a shop – from her mother and elder brother to her father and mother-in-law. Bengali women from respectable families did not do such things, she was told. But her husband was on her side. In fact, it was because of him, for him, that she was doing this. It was he who wanted her in the shop. And he had his way, especially since he had already done something wilder – sent his wife to Japan! All in the service of photography, of course.

✦✦✦

Sakhi mashi told me the Japan story in short. But by now I was eager to know mesho's version as well – not just about Japan, but his side of the THE NEW FOTOLAB story. He was out of town that day, so I went to the shop a second time (a few weeks later) to talk to him.

He was the one who was passionate about photography. His father wanted him to have a stable job, which working at the Reserve Bank of India secured for him, but the photography bug just would not go. So, he went for a Diploma course, then taught in the evenings at the Dum Dum Motijhil College (affiliated to Calcutta University), where he came under the tutelage of none other than the legendary Benu Sen. From the very beginning, he loved doing portraits, and got the opportunity to exhibit his work a couple of times. His work was appreciated, alright, but he could not sell any of it. In fact, he spent money trying to promote those exhibitions. That was when he was advised to open a studio of his own, to do his work professionally and to be able to earn from it. He promptly took that advice, borrowed money from his father, and opened THE NEW FOTOLAB in 1978. He married Sakhi mashi two years later.

Soon after their marriage, he got a rare chance: he was selected by 'Minolta' to get a six-month photography training in Japan, but RBI did not allow him leave (even when he was willing to go without pay) because it argued, the training would not value-add to his banking job. Mesho could not afford to leave his job, so he asked 'Minolta' if his wife could go instead. She will have to prove her credentials, was the response. Mashi was willing to give up her job at 'Johnson & Johnson' to go to Japan, but she had absolutely no idea about photography. Hence, as always, she just did the needful: quickly learnt the ropes in a crash course and earned herself the traineeship on behalf of her husband. Mesho's father told him, "Your wife will never come back". But she did! And helped him set up a complete colour studio in 1984.

It has been going strong ever since. The studio has evolved in tandem with all the changes in the world of photography – from black and white to colour photography to videography (late 80s/90s) to the digital revolution (2000 onwards), with mobile-phone cameras giving their business the toughest challenge since 2010.

But the technical aspects apart, mashi-mesho's journey as a couple took a new turn in 1996 when mesho gave up his Reserve Bank job. There was a major reason for it: that year, THE NEW FOTOLAB got involved with the work of the Election Commission (under T.N. Seshan) – they did Electoral Roll

Preparation, Voter ID Cards; in fact, they were the only agency in Kolkata to have a complete set-up to do this work. They first worked for the Government of West Bengal (Hoogly district), and then for the Governments of Assam and Tripura as well. Sakhi mashi couldn't handle it all alone. That is when mesho joined her.

Ever since, they have been in their shop together – every working day of their lives, from morning to night.

On my way back from THE NEW FOTOLAB the evening I talked to mesho, I suddenly remembered a small detail – a photograph that used to be placed on the refrigerator in the living room of the small apartment that I had frequented as a child. It was of them as a newlywed couple: laughing into the camera, they had arms around each other's necks in a gesture more of comradeship than youthful romance. No coy bride and protective groom there. Just partners. Their relationship has remained that way for 40 years!

A DIFFERENT KIND OF HOLI (23 March 2019)

So what, I was in the hospital? I was made to play Holi, too!

I was very unwell throughout January this year and was diagnosed with multiple problems in February – acute colitis, gall bladder stones and fibroids in the uterus. I knew something was wrong in my body, but was shocked to find so many organs in disorder! Mid-February to mid-March, I went through a flurry of specialist consultations and medical investigations. For most of February, I was under medication and underwent a colonoscopy early in March. Thankfully, there was nothing major to worry about. But the gallstone surgery had to happen and the gall bladder was removed. That happened on 20th March. I was back home on the 22nd, with one organ less in my body and four incisions across my tummy.

S had come to meet me during 'Visiting Hours' on the 20th (after her dad had secured "special permission"), a hand-made card in her hand. In between horizontal bars of colours, it said: "Mamma, please return soon, and next year I hope no one has to go to the hospital. Happy Holi". I was struck by the long sentence (and the fact that there was not a single spelling mistake in it)! S loves to draw and gifts me a card every few days, for all manner of reasons; a lot of them periodic declarations of her love: "I love you, Mamma". They await me especially on evenings I am late in returning home... her way of saying she has missed me after school. They melt my heart, unfailingly!

But what was really unusual about this particular card was that she was referring to something else, a painful memory from last year. Last Holi, my father was almost dying in the hospital with a freak kidney failure that no nephrologist could make sense of; this Holi, I had my gall bladder removed. Both years, S got to enjoy Holi with her dad, but the shadow of this thing called 'hospital' stayed in her mind. And made its way into her card.

On the morning of Holi, I reflected on this – on how Holi has seemed to have taken on a new association after my return to India. But even as I did so, a bevy of nurses and attendants, all laughter and youthful joy, came rushing in to my room with colours and sweets and made me feel special. I was touched. I will cherish that moment.

There is something I will cherish even more. I was told by her dad that evening that the previous night, just before going to sleep, S had confessed to him: "Papa, I love you very much. But I love Mamma a little more". I think my surgery was totally worth it!

DEAR ANNA (27 March 2019)

Many happy returns of the day, Anna!

You always remember to forget my birthday – I thought of reminding that to you on yours!

I feel a dull ache within me every time I think of you, Anna. I don't know when we will meet again. Or, if ever. Our paths have no reason to cross.

I cannot imagine why you would want to come to Kolkata, and I certainly do not belong to the minuscule, highly privileged class of globe-trotting, continent-hopping, jet-setting individuals who can travel to another continent just to meet a friend. Forget international travel, even travelling within India is expensive for me; and given the kind of job that I do, and the fact that I have had to restart my career right from scratch after relocating back to India, I actually just about manage to cover the necessary expenses. Things may change in the future... but for now, this is the reality.

There was so much that bound us together, Anna – our shared passion for writing, our experience of motherhood, our heartaches. Any one of these would have been enough for a lasting bond!

Though we had known each other in Amsterdam from late 2008, from our 'Mezrab' days, it was not until 2012 that we became intimate. And how! Till then, there was this healthy respect for each other's writing, a mutual attraction of sorts, which, before it could bloom, was cut short by the German interlude in my life in 2009. When I had left for Stuttgart, Pippo was a toddler;

when I returned to Amsterdam and got in touch with our writing group again, you had another baby (Juno) in your arms. And the venue of the group had shifted from the Iranian cafe to your lovely 'Zolder'.

I just loved those critique sessions in your attic. They were almost always a full house – with Eric, Chris, David, Ben, Tori, Smruthy, you and me. We got better acquainted during that time – both as aspiring writers and individuals. But it was S's birth that really changed the dynamic of our relationship. Not her birth, actually, but the time and circumstance. I was off the writing group, once again, soon after re-joining it. You were full of concern for me and came to visit me often... and then we opened up to each other in a way we had not thought possible before. Our friendship blossomed that summer.

The sharing of heartaches, emotional losses and the challenges of motherhood were such a potent combination. And we shared all of that mostly in my living room and in our walks in Buitenveldert, moving through a dense green canopy of trees. I can still picture us in my mind's eye: you walking with your bike, your hands on the handlebars; me walking beside you. We are engrossed in conversation. Sometimes we are quiet, just drinking in the beauty of the lush green of summer, with a soft breeze in our hair, the delicate touch of the late-afternoon sun on our skin.

You and your bike, Anna- inseparable! You rode down to my place in every season—spring and summer in those breezy frocks, autumn and winter bundled from head to toe. But ride you did, through it all—that's the Dutch in you, through and through.

In your company, cultural differences melted away... the way you understood me, my mind, my writing. We came from radically different backgrounds: you had roamed the world with your diplomat parents, studied in different countries, pursued creative writing seriously, lived with your partner and became a mother pretty early in your relationship. Mine had been an essentially cocooned and boring middle-class upbringing, mostly confined to one city, where I continued to live and work doggedly after marriage, till the point I decided to leave my academic career in India and join my husband in Amsterdam - to have the kind of life together that did not seem possible in Kolkata. In Amsterdam, I came to writing tentatively, taking years to gather up the courage to admit to myself its importance in my life. And my marriage was worlds away from your partnership in every way, not the least in the time it took us to be parents. And yet, Anna, how we connected! – our Dutch and Indian selves totally oblivious of their national identities in the face of female bonding!

The irony was that, for a long time, I actually thought you were British because of your distinct Brit accent. Only much later did I learn that that is because you had spent a substantial part of your school and university years in the UK.

S was born in Amsterdam and spent her first five years there. And though there were quite a few frequent visitors among my friends - my chanting group (Jaya in particular, in the first two years); also, Anindita - you are the only one whom she saw consistently for all those five years. And with whom she spent time (in however small doses) more or less regularly. She loved your company! That wonderful way you have with children. I remember the times when both of us, mum and daughter, fought for your attention – with me trying to discuss something or the other and she eager to show off her latest toys or doodles.

I regret the fact that I never got the chance to spend much time with Pippo and Juno. And yet, I feel, I know them well. I have heard so much about them from you. Your immense patience with and brutal honesty about both your children are qualities I have always marvelled at and learnt much from.

And I have always found your presence so reassuring: be it my writerly confusions or motherly worries (which I had an awful lot in S's initial years) or my eternal existential anxieties, you were always so comforting with your words – your responses invariably compassionate, and yet pragmatic. No 'advice' ever, just distilled wisdom framed in quotidian terms.

The only aspect about you that I found difficult to deal with was the way you sometimes vanished from the face of the earth without notice. Camping somewhere in France or Belgium, or generally, just unavailable. I initially found those sudden silences - especially after times of great camaraderie - unnerving, but with time, I learnt to simply wait out those phases. You, too, relented a bit later, sometimes letting me know that you would be away.

The special relationship that was initiated between us in 2012 grew in depth. In the next five years, the last two/three being the most memorable. Especially, 2017. My imminent return to India added an altogether different piquancy to our meetings. We met more often than ever before. Could not have enough of each other. And till the last moment, I remember, neither of us could bring ourselves to believe that we were actually parting.

I will never forget the moment of our last goodbye, Anna - at 'Le Pain Quotidien' - when I waved at you, you waved back, both with forced smiles, and then your bike turned right from Gelderlandplein, taking you away from me forever.

'Le Pain Quotidien' – those early morning teas we had there in the last months, after dropping off the kids to school, are the ones I remember and miss the most. Other people still meet there, don't they? With the morning light pouring in through those long glass doors, the sun warming them and their conversations. How I envy them, Anna... friends who can continue to meet!

I do not know when I will meet you again, Anna. I do not even know when we will talk again. In 20 months, there has been just one freak phone call between us. Maybe we will manage to talk again sooner this time. Maybe not. But I will always love you. And cherish the times we have shared. And... think of you with a dull ache in my heart!

"WAITING FOR YOU" (11 May 2019)

Ma does not come in my dreams. She absolutely refused in the initial months after her death in August 2016. Then she relented a little. She came in all about five times in my dreams – five times in a year and a half. After that, for a whole year, I did not count. Because the few flimsy appearances she made in all that time - always hovering on the fringes of the scene unfolding in my mind - did not count for much. In life, she was right at the centre of my existence; after death, she was unwilling to play even a bit-part. As I say, she has utterly and completely abandoned me.

Not so with her first-born. She visits didi (my elder sister) regularly. I understand that that is because didi thinks of Ma more often than I do and probably misses her more than me. I certainly do not believe that Ma favours her after death because she loves Ma more than me – *that* I am not willing to concede.

It is no surprise then - given how jilted I feel - that the dream about Ma that I remember the most is actually not mine, but one that didi had seen once and had described to me in great detail over the phone, sobbing the entire time.

Didi's dream

This is what she saw: She is coming home from school on our school bus. She gets down at the Hudco crossing in Ultadanga. She expects to see Ma, but Ma is not there. She is confused. She looks around, scouring the faces of pedestrians and people waiting to board buses. But no, Ma is not in the crowd. She waits for a while... her heart beating slightly faster now. Still, no sign of Ma. She now hops onto the Ultadanga bridge, an unknown fear gripping her belly, and impelling her feet to speed up; so that before she knows, she has already crossed the bridge, and come down on the other side, facing Kankurgachi, just before 'Uttarapan' – just as she does with Ma every day (though at a much more relaxed pace). She is now not so much going home as going in search of Ma. But before she can jump out of the last leg of stairs and into the pavement, as she is wont to, lo and behold... there is Ma, sitting just at the point she is about to jump from, her head slightly bent. "What happened? Where were you? I was looking for you...", didi is almost screaming now, shock and anger and relief pouring forth in equal measure. Ma does not seem to mind her rude behaviour (otherwise unacceptable to her). She simply looks up at didi and says, in a tone of infinite sadness: "I was waiting for you".

Didi was inconsolable after seeing that dream, because there was a paradox there: the body and face that she saw in the dream was of our younger mother, the mother of two pre-pubescent girls, but the voice was much older. It was the voice, with its particular tone of sadness, that we heard over phone calls – continents away, decades later. Didi's dream had thus made two moments, from completely different times in our lives, immanent in each other. Central to it was waiting. And that voice? In time, that voice would override/overwhelm every other memory associated with Ma – because that is practically all we had of her in the last ten years of her life. She had, in effect, become a voice to us.

When didi recounted the dream to me, while hearing this part - the waiting part - a shiver ran down my spine, remembering another mother-daughter story. "Waiting for you"... what could it mean? Oh God! then I checked myself. I did not tell anything to didi.

Letting/Not letting go

The story that I decided not to tell didi was a story that a dear friend of mine (B) had shared with me. About another friend of hers. A mother-daughter story – the strangest bonding I have ever heard of. She shared it with me to console me soon after Ma's death – when I told her of how bereft I felt that I could not talk to Ma even in dreams. "Your mother has liberated you", my friend had said, "let you go, so that you can lead your own life". We usually talk of "letting go" from the survivor's perspective, the one who is left behind after the death of a dear one. We are supposed to "let go" of the dead. But B was saying something else: the dead also need to "let go" of the living. While this seems/sounds obvious, not all do. Like the mother of this friend of B.

B's friend, P, and her mother, were exceptionally close. Had always been. B not only knew it, but had also witnessed it herself many times when she visited P's home. P and her mother were both academics, though in different disciplines - one was a doctorate in Bengali literature, the other in Linguistics - and shared a strong intellectual bond, apart from their filial relationship. P's mother died in late 2016. P was distraught, and in her grief, would even neglect her small child. She would often see her mother in her home in Bangalore (where the latter had been a frequent visitor). One day, after returning home from the office, even her husband saw her mother sitting quietly on their couch, in a gesture of waiting. He was petrified. But he did not share his experience with his wife, wanting to spare her further perturbation. P fell ill soon after with pneumonia and had to be admitted to a hospital. She missed her mother. But maybe her mother missed her even more. For, when her condition deteriorated and it became necessary to put her on a ventilator, she refused it, saying: "Ma is here to take me, my time has come". And that is indeed what happened: P left this world to join her mother on the other side of life.

It is the eeriest of stories that I have ever heard. Can a mother snatch away her daughter like that? Miss her so much that she cannot allow her to live? Be totally unconcerned about the daughter's husband and child? I don't know. Most mothers, even when they share a strong bond, seem to want nothing more than their daughters settling down well with their partners (and children). P's mum was certainly an exception!

Hearing that story really consoled me in 2016. Despite my grief, I certainly preferred being liberated/ left behind, and I remember I had felt both relieved and reassured that my mother had "let go" of me. Relieved, because it was such a scary story; reassured, because it was in sync with my mother's selfless character. She had had enough of life. She had said her goodbye, and now just wanted to leave us in peace with our own pursuits and passions.

That consolation of 2016, however, did not last long for me – for before long, I again craved to see Ma in a dream; craved desperately to talk to her, hear her voice. She would not come to me. So, I would avidly hear didi's dreams.

Waiting

That dream of didi's that I remember the most took us back to our school days – when Ma used to wait for us. She would go to Ultadanga (from our flat in Kankurgachi, a ten-minute walk) to pick us up, in order to save 40/50 minutes of our time on our way back from school. Reason? Our school bus picked us up earliest in the morning and dropped us last in the afternoon, after taking a detour from Ultadanga-Hudco and dropping all the girls in Salt Lake. How unfair!

Ma wanted to give us relief, decrease a bit of our fatigue. She was so completely given over to being our mother! And always and ever, she waited for us: waited for us to come home from school, then from college and university. Every waiting had a distinct flavour: in the school phase, it was in happy anticipation of sharing our day, our new learnings and excitements; in the college/university phase, it was more like waiting for two friends to come home and join her for a chat over evening tea. But that gave way to an altogether different kind of waiting when we both left home in 1999 (me for another home after marriage, didi for another city), and then the country in 2006/2007. That waiting was from an empty nest – waiting to see me once a week or fortnight, didi once a year; then, with a tremendous longing, waiting to have us together at home once a year, sometimes once in two years for a few days.

By the time we left home in 1999, Ma had no friends left in her life but us. The constraints of the life that she had chosen for herself after leaving her career did not allow such luxuries. There were siblings, relatives, and acquaintances galore, of course – but those were more ties of duty and obligation, or had to do with the maintenance of civil social relations. There were moments of congeniality - even conviviality - in those interactions, but they were not equivalent to the presence of a friend, with whom Ma could share her interests or really open up her heart. Ma had an active life of the mind: she read and wrote, watched KBC with a pen and paper in hand (always jotting down new information), and occasionally saw films which she would then discuss with me over the phone. She was also engaged for a substantial part of the day with domestic chores, which she insisted on doing herself till the last day of her life; but the beating heart of her daily routine was gone. Her life revolved around us for two-and-a-half decades; when we left, it was never the same again for her. She never wanted us back in Kolkata after we left - she genuinely respected our individual trajectories - but she sorely missed us. And waited to see us!

I remembered this waiting.... and then I understood the true meaning of "I was waiting for you".

You waited for us, Ma, for so long – year in and year out. And now, when I have come back, you are no more. There is so much that I need to tell you... so much... but no, I will not talk to you. It is now a proven fact that you love didi more than me!

UDICHI OLD AGE HOME (14 May 2019)

Everyone who could has left. Almost all the children. More than half of the 32 flats of UDICHI - the 'Co-operative Housing Society' in Kankurgachi, North Kolkata, where my sister and I grew up - are now peopled either by ageing couples or by widows/widowers. Every year, their numbers increase. Every year, when one more dead body is taken away by an ambulance, the elderly form a shrinking circle of grief – offering flowers to the departed, paying their last respects with bowed heads and stooped shoulders, and lisping quiet commiserations to the surviving partner.

Most of their children have left home - for better study or work opportunities, or else marriage - some in other cities in India (Bangalore, Pune, Delhi); many in other countries/continents (the UK, USA, Australia, the Netherlands); a few have returned but are settled in other parts of the city with their own children and spouses.

When my family started living here in 1978, the age group of our friends spanned the entire school-going years – right from play-school toddlers to those appearing for their boards. And every year, there would be someone appearing for their boards, or clearing medical/engineering entrance exams, or graduating. We - 21 girls and 22 boys in all - represented a long continuum of learning (read 'exams'). Then there was a long continuum of leaving UDICHI – for all the reasons enumerated above. Followed by (for most) getting married and having children of our own. Till that point, till the new generation came along, we saw the flow of life through our lives – our education, careers, marriage and kids. That another generation - that of our parents

- was simultaneously getting older and frailer, it hit us only when the deaths started happening pretty regularly. Initially at a slow pace, but at times striking like an epidemic – like the year my mother left us, when three women of Block-B (including her) passed away within eight months.

Our parents, like us, also represent a wide range – age-wise. The elderly of UDICHI can be anywhere between their early 60s and late 80s. With their children roughly aged between the mid-30s and late-50s. The younger set among the old is, of course, still faring well. Most lead active retired lives, spending time doing household work, buying groceries, cooking, gardening, going for morning/evening walks. Some travel frequently and have visiting children whom they also visit in turn. With those having kids in the same city, a lot of their social time revolves around their grandchildren. It is the really old with children far away who lead the loneliest lives, and who perforce have had to be the strongest, both in terms of resilience and resourcefulness.

Teachers, new brides, mothers and matriarchs

One of the unique things about UDICHI was that it was full of teachers – school, college, university. You name it. The most respected among them was undoubtedly the late Dr. Triguna Sen – the first VC of Jadavpur University, who had also been Union Minister for Education and a member of the Rajya Sabha. Dr. Sen lived here for a while with his elder daughter, who taught Philosophy at Lady Brabourne. Actually, between us students and the many teachers of UDICHI, we covered most of the major institutions of Kolkata (and some from outside it): from Patha Bhavan and Holy Child to Calcutta Girls/Boys, Loreto and

Auxilium, from Presidency and Brabourne to Surendranath and Basantidevi, from Calcutta and Jadavpur University to CMC, RG Kar and ISI. Hardly surprising, then, that most of us fared well academically, the importance of high scores in middle-class existence having been dinned into our heads pretty early in life.

Among the parents, whether teachers or not, there were informal groups that were clearly discernible even to us children. One was a group of men of roughly the same age, teaching in different colleges, all of whom started their careers in the same decade and retired a few years of each other. They had one sort of camaraderie. Completely different was another kind of bonding among a group of young women who had come in as new brides to UDICHI – all in the year 1979-1980. Three, in particular - Manjula, Mithu and Minku kakima (three M's!) - were very close. They were all good-looking and dressed very well. There were also four/five other not-so-new brides, who were a little older than them, having married just before coming here or just slightly before the younger ones. The biggest group, by far, were mothers – who constantly kept themselves updated about what the others' children were doing and invariably found them better/smarter/brighter/more talented than their own! At the other end of the mothers, was a tiny group of the elderly – matriarchs/ patriarchs of a few joint families in the complex. The overwhelming majority, however, were nuclear families, many of whom had previously belonged to a joint setup (like my parents).

These groups, usually meeting randomly within the building premises while going out or coming from somewhere, would become self-evident on Sarawati Puja – the day that UDICHI truly came alive, annually. All groups and sub-groups among parents would just not leave each other's company that day. For us children, it was the most eagerly awaited moment of the year, and it remained so throughout our school years. (It dampened somewhat after that). We were usually all excitement not only for the puja and the delicious communal lunch and dinner that were an integral part of it, but primarily for the cultural program that we put up every year. For which we would rehearse for months.

Bhola kaku and Pradip kaku

I had my favourite 'kakus' and 'kakimas' (uncles and aunts) while growing up in UDICHI. Of them, Bhola kaku topped the list. He was a Professor of Chemistry at Ramakrishna Mission Vivekananda Centenary College, Rahara, in North 24 Parganas. His wife taught the same subject at Lady Brabourne College in Kolkata. They both happen to be avid readers and lovers of literature. While I waited for the school bus in the morning, especially in my secondary years, kaku would stand and chat with me about books and authors. The one recommendation of his that I particularly remember from that time was Irving Stone's *Lust for Life*. I was in class IX, and knew nothing about either the author or his subject then. But I was so mesmerized by the book that I promptly followed it up with *The Agony and the Ecstasy*, *Depths of Glory*, and later, *The Passions of the Mind*.

Bhola kaku is a stoic. No matter what he is going through in his life, he has the same smile on his face and speaks in the same tone of mock-banter whenever he meets me. His 'me-time' is 11 pm, when reclining on the railing of his balcony, he silently ruminates in the dark, cigarette in hand. I have seen that as a child and teenager, as a young adult, while visiting my parents after marriage, during short annual trips from Amsterdam. I see it even now after returning home.

Bhola kaku has a son, who, after graduate studies in the US, now lives and works in Bangalore. His closest friend is Pradip kaku, who is among the very few parents in UDICHI who are not alone: his only son, recently married, stays with him. Pradip kaku is one of the quietest persons I have met in my life. Unlike Bhola kaku, I did not have much interaction with him when I was growing up; and his principal identity for me was that he had a beautiful wife! - Mithu kakima - one of the kindest and sweetest women I have known, part of the trio of new brides I just mentioned.

Pradip kaku is the current Secretary of UDICHI. Bhola kaku had held that post before him for a long time. Between them, they keep the co-operative going. Though of course there is a General Body of 'Members of the Society' (comprising of owners of the flats) that meets every few months, as well as a six-member Managing Committee within the GB, everyone knows that if there is any work to be done, than those are the two men that one has to turn to: whether it is getting the gardens behind all the three Blocks spruced up, or the water-tank cleaned, or sundry little requirements like getting hold of the housing-sweeper for extra work, etc.

For their age, Bhola kaku and Pradip kaku look remarkably young. And they look more or less the same as they did 15 years back. No exaggeration there! One of the secrets of their young-looking, slim selves is their daily walk – a ritual that they have kept up with religious regularity. Come rain or shine, you are sure to see the two walking out of the building around 11 am, going to have tea in a 'para' (neighbourhood) stall.

It is a blessing at their age to have a friend nearby. And nothing like if he lives next door. Well, Bhola kaku and Pradip kaku have been next-door neighbours on the first floor of Block-A for 40 years now. I never want that to end. I never want UDICHI to have any other association for 11 am than them walking out together to have tea!

AN ASPIRATIONAL FAMILY (6 June 2019)

Kuheli (name changed) comes to look after my child, leaving her own. My daughter is seven, her son is nine. Mine goes to an international school, the first in the city (est. 1953); hers goes to Hare School, one of the oldest (est.1818) and most prestigious schools of not only Calcutta, but Bengal. S going to an international school is no big surprise – given that she came to Kolkata after her first five years in Amsterdam, where she went to an international school. Her very difficult transition from one continent to another, two years back, was thus made slightly easier, at least on the school front. But Kuheli's son, Bablu (name changed), going to Hare School is really a big deal – given that she studied till standard IV and her driver husband till standard VII. It is her husband who insisted on it, she says, and it is where her son has been studying since standard I. He is now in standard III.

Kuheli grew up in the Sunderbans and frankly detested studies. Her parents did not force it upon her. Third among five siblings, her match with her husband, Asim (name changed) was made through an aunt. It was considered a very good match – a driver with a stable monthly income who lived with his parents and grandmother in a respectable locality of North Calcutta. She is now in her late-20s, but looks much younger, with an innocence writ large on her face that even 11+ years of marriage, domesticity, motherhood and life in the city has not been able to tarnish. She is of middling height, slim, with big eyes and long hair. This last won my daughter's heart right from day-1. And the fact that she has a smartphone. They both watch videos on it on the sly - with all the excitement of a forbidden pleasure - despite the taboo I have placed on it. Or rather, because of it. S cannot access my phone easily. Not to be deterred, she has thus made a secret ally of her nanny. And successfully!

But Kuheli's phone - like that of all working mothers, across the class divide - is a very essential tool for her: for remotely tackling problems at home, exchanging texts with her husband, constantly checking on her son's whereabouts. She has a lot to check on because her son has a chock-a-bloc routine. His school hours are from 6.00 to 10.30 am. But his studies do not end there. In fact, that is only the beginning. After returning home from school, 11.00-12.30 is spent with a tutor (who is a college student herself). Another such instalment happens from 7.30-9.00 pm – this time outside home, at another tutor's place, on the same street, where he goes alone. So, at age 9, B spends 4.5 hours at school and 3 hours outside it – studying! Every day, except Sunday. Mondays and Tuesdays, he also goes for drawing class – 90 minutes each, just before his evening tuitions. That is also in the neighbourhood, but is chaperoned by the granny, as it involves crossing a street. Besides study-tuitions and drawing classes, swimming was also on the agenda last year. But logistics stood in the way – none could pick/drop him at the allotted hours. But Kuheli is determined. Those classes, too, would begin - she told me the other day - once the school timings changed. A different algorithm of routines would then make it possible.

Kuheli and her husband are very clear in their minds as to why Bablu has to undergo such a gruelling schedule from such a tender age. "Oke to manush hote hobe, boudi" (He will have to grow up to be an educated man) – she had told me simply, when I had asked. Admission in a good school was thus of paramount importance, and since they themselves cannot guide his education, they decided to hire teachers to do it for them. Right from primary school – a good start was important – both were on the same page on this. Costs had to be met somehow... hence Kuheli's joining as a nanny last year.

This is her first job – the first time that she has ever stepped out of home, outside the roles of a daughter, daughter-in-law, wife and mother. She would actually still prefer to be at home – as she cannot give any time to her child beyond getting him ready in the morning, picking him from school (both rushed affairs), and having dinner at night (when she is utterly exhausted for anything beyond functional talk). Also, because this job imposes upon her a double labour – do ALL the housework (just as before) AND work as a nanny. Her only respite is that she has genuinely bonded with the child she has been entrusted with. And having innocent fun with her charge in the afternoon makes it all bearable...!

CHUMKI MAIMA (7 June 2019)

Today, a childhood memory of mine suddenly resurfaced – that of a wedding I had attended in early June 1983.

It was the wedding of one of my mother's cousins, and I remember it mostly because of the bride! Her name was 'Chumki', and true to the name, she sparkled! Honest to God, I had never seen any creature as beautiful as her! She was my first love! Married to Ma's brightest younger cousin, she became an instant favourite with us and Ma's darling. And for her, Ma became a cross between an elder sister and a mother figure (Ma was much older than her husband, Goutam). In the huge new family that she got married into, with its army of doting relatives, Chumki maima somehow clung only to Ma. Felt safe with her, could be herself with her.

We were super excited when Ma's 'chhoto kaka' and 'kakima', the youngest paternal uncle and aunt, came to give the wedding card. The bride-to-be was just 18 – a first-year Philosophy Honours student at Bethune College. But more interestingly, she was a Kathak dancer whom we had already seen on TV. Who knew she would become our aunt? The groom was 24. He was our golden boy: fresh from IIT-Kharagpur, with already a foreign work stint in Japan. He was short, slim and fair. So was she. They looked like two dolls together. But she was beautiful! I had seen marriages galore on Ma's side of the family – but the kind of excitement and anticipation that this one had generated was unparalleled. Chumki maima was married in her own house in Baghbajar - on the terrace - on the fourth floor. We had lost our breath by the time we reached up. The rose water with which we had been sprinkled as welcome had already evaporated by then and we had started to sweat. But we forgot everything the moment we entered the terrace. People were jostling to see the bride, with 'oohs' and 'aahs' and 'bah-bahs' all round. "Eki pori na apsara"? (Is she a fairy or a celestial nymph?) Boro-mama, my eldest maternal uncle, asked – a middle-aged man whom everyone respected, now struck with wonder. I stared at her with an open mouth. She smiled equally on everyone – very much like Browning's Duchess! And like the Duke, I already felt jealous about the others!!

This is a Beng-lish song that a maternal cousin of the groom (nicknamed, 'Babuji') composed. It was a huge hit, and we all sang it with gusto:

Babuji-দা is Engineer,

বৌদি the great Kathak dancer,

Engineer আর dancer মিলে করে ফেললো বিয়ে,

আমরা সবাই কামনা করি, থেকো তোমরা সুখী ।

Babuji-da Japan-e গিয়ে, একটি Japan-i কে নিয়ে,

Ballroom-e dance করতে গিয়ে, পিছলে পড়লো তাকে সাথে নিয়ে,

হায় রে পোড়া কপাল Babuji-দার,

Promise করলো করবে না সে dance আর,

মনে পড়লো Chumki বৌদির কথা,

শোনো শোনো শোনো শোনো শোনো – Babuji-দার কান্ড।

Ma belongs to a huge brood. Her father was the eldest of 19 siblings – ten brothers, nine sisters. And all of them had at least three/four children. The youngest - the groom's father - had three; the groom being the eldest. These boys were nicknamed 'tin ratna' (three jewels), by which was meant that all of them had gone on to study engineering at JU and IIT – the ultimate destination for any Bengali boy of merit.

This wedding was special, and people had gathered not only from all parts of West Bengal, but also from Delhi and Dhaka. It was huge fun for us children. I generally lapped up all the fun – except for the inconvenience of the bathroom. I have always been finicky about it. Relatives filled all three floors of Ma's ancestral family house in Ballygunge. And three huge buses were rented to take the 'bor jatri' (marriage party) from one end of Calcutta to another, from Ballygunge (in the south) to Baghbajar (in the north). That was an adventure in itself! The bus stood waiting as the women kept on with their 'sajgoj' – their Benarasi saris and gold jewellery, and flowers on their elaborate 'khopas' (buns). There was a budding romance among a pair of close relatives that was much whispered about... the young aunt in question took the longest time to dress!

After the wedding, all the nights were devoted by Ma and her huge gang of cousins to major trips down memory lane. They would sit up late into the night - all lying on each other in one huge loop - and talk and laugh till the wee hours of the morning. Teasing each other and making the children listen to all their stories: collective memories of their 'desher bari' in what is now Bangladesh, with dozens of cousins growing up in the lap of nature… they would reminiscence nostalgically about this tree, that pond, a particular maid or servant, uncle or aunt; and above all, about their beloved 'Thakuma', paternal grandmother – far more than their grandfather. I have heard a lot of stories about her from Ma: she was a true matriarch, who kept the whole family together and managed to love and be loved by everyone. Daughter of a jail super and a matric of that age, how she managed to bear 19 children and yet live healthy till a ripe old age, surviving some of her own children, is an enduring mystery to me.

That wedding was perhaps the fifth full-scale wedding that I had attended in my nine years of life. Hence, by then, I knew all the rituals associated with Bengali weddings, the most painful of which was, of course, the 'kone bidai' – farewell to the bride as she left her natal home for her husband's. Ever since a small girl, I cried in every 'bidai', though I understood little of what it meant. An uncle of mine, totally flabbergasted by all the crying that was going on as he took his bride home, said: "You feel as if you are stealing away the daughter". He was right, of course!

In this wedding, however, the bride was coming into our house. So, we were filled with joy and anticipation. We had all fallen in love with her beauty – and her spontaneous sweetness. She was polite and yet warm to old and young alike – with just the right mix of deference for elders and affection for the young. No artifice. No putting on airs. No arrogance about her beauty. She carried the weight of all that attention and admiration with admirable ease; she was very comfortable with her beauty and unassuming.

Her furniture arrived before her. The usual stuff that all brides' families were supposed to give and which both the parties took for granted, not deeming it as 'dowry': just essential stuff to start off one's domestic life with – bed, almirah, dressing-table, *alnah*. In her case, things were a little different: she had been given two single beds by her family instead of a double one (which were then joined as one); and two almirahs, one each for the bride and groom, which was rare. The best piece of furniture, however (to my eyes), was a triple-faced mirror, with two half-oval glasses closing in on a rectangular one.

All the young men of the house worked the whole day to get the furniture together, looking just a bunch of well-fed *mistris* in their white *bunyans* and *lungis*! The temperature was soaring high and they sweated as if they had a bath. The biggest room in the house had been given to the new couple. It had been freshly painted and had new curtains. The room was completely transformed by the time the bride arrived.

I was a slip of a girl then, just nine years old; but I distinctly remember feeling: "amar kobe hobe" (When will this happen to me)?!

DOCTOR and PATIENT (8 June 2019)

He comes punctually at 9 am to the Kolkata Municipal Corporation (KMC) office in Kankurgachi – Ward no. 32, under Borough III. He has been a 'Medical Officer' since 2006, though at this particular ward only from 2015. The Ward is located on the ground floor of a two-storied blue building, adjacent to a park. A spanking new and more spacious building is coming up right next to it, where the office is slated to shift in another year or two. But the current outfit is small. The entrance has a lobby where patients wait. One has to turn left to access the main office. As one enters that corridor, one finds little rooms allocated to different 'departments': on the left are the 'Immunization' and 'Waste Management' departments; on the right, the 'Electrical' and 'Health' departments; and at the very end, the medical laboratory. The Health Department has two divisions – the doctor's chamber and the medical officer's administrative office. Here, the two functions are fused into one – or rather, squeezed into one little room. With files and papers overflowing everywhere, there is just enough space for doctor and patient to sit facing each other. The stream of patients is endless, mostly from the nearby slums, who come for free treatment and medicine. It seemed to me, in a brief half-hour visit, that they do not come until things are really bad. Sample this: a little girl with a 'perek' (nail) in her foot that has been allowed to stay there for two days; a middle-aged woman with high fever for five days; a man with stomach upset for three days. It seemed the poor are wary of taking free service – but it was just one part of the story, I later learnt from the doctor. Many of the patients who come to him are actually quite aware of the medical services that they can avail of at his KMC ward, and do not waste any time to do so! But either way, to spend several hours every morning in this office must be a daily lesson in the ground realities of the state of health of the urban poor. I am sure it keeps the doctor grounded.

I recently took an appointment with the doctor in question - Saurabh Basu - at his KMC office to witness first-hand this side of his profession. It is a side I was not even aware of till a few months back. I knew the private Nursing Homes he is associated with, in one of which my mother had died. In fact, for a long time, the only association of him that I had in my mind was that: he was the only doctor who was available on a stormy evening in August 2016 when my mother had a sudden, severe cerebral attack and my octogenarian father was at a loss for what to do. But for Saurabh's prompt presence, the ambulance would have been out of bounds for Baba. Ma did not survive the attack. She went into a coma the very next day, was brain-dead the second day and finally her heart gave way on the third. There was nothing much that we could do. But what Saurabh had done, I can never forget: even if I had not met him ever again in my life, I would have been eternally grateful to him for that one evening, when he was by my father's side.

Saurabh's association with my parents had started a couple of years before that, when both didi and I lived abroad. I had heard about him from Ma – about a young doctor who sometimes came to see her at home. Ma's health had deteriorated since we had left. But she was very reluctant to visit doctors or take medicines. Especially since she seemed to manage her daily routine pretty well without them. This was, however, a sore point with Baba: they had endless fights over this, and Baba would frequently complain about it over the phone to both us daughters. (Ma too had her bagful of bitter complaints - of a different kind - against Baba. We heard them both. Scolded them both, by turns, from thousands of miles away. Nothing changed. They continued being themselves). But sometimes in the later years, when Ma fell very ill, it was genuinely difficult for her to visit a clinic – as most of them involved quite a bit of walking and crossing a dangerous junction. House-visits of GPs were the only option left then. But the two GPs we had were out of reach: one had recently died, and in any case, being a very senior doctor, he never came home; the other, much younger, did, at first – but after a while, his private practice became so successful that he had no time for visiting patients at all. Enter Saurabh. Who lived and worked (at least for part of the day) close to our building. And - a very important 'and' – had a compassionate heart!

It is solely because of this quality that his relationship has endured with my father – after he became a widower. Baba was doing fine in the first year after Ma's death. But in February/March 2018, he had a freak kidney failure that kept him five weeks in the ICU and almost took his life. Luckily, he survived, but he has been a shadow of himself ever since: frail, his (almost mythical) confidence shaken, his health unpredictable, and his mental condition eternally panicky and anxious. After several bedridden months, post his hospitalization, he has been back on his feet, but he keeps suffering from some ailment or the other. Often, he thinks them to be more than what they are. And when in distress, he calls Saurabh, requesting him to pay a visit. Saurabh obliges – unfailingly! He is very patient with this patient of his! It must be said on Baba's behalf that he is very meticulous and methodical. He keeps everything ready before Saurabh's visit: all his problems are listed, point-wise, in a paper; followed by queries about medicines, similarly listed; followed by the most recent blood reports, chronologically arranged. All this, "to make the most effective use of time". But the actual elaboration invariably goes contrary to the plan! If I happen to be present during such a visit, I just lose my cool. But the doctor does not. In fact, he even indulges in a bit of a chat with his patient!

This patient-friendliness, he told me, he has imbibed from his own father - Dr. Siddhartha Kumar Basu - who inspired the son to join his profession. Basu Sr. was not only a good doctor/ gynaecologist, but also a far-sighted professional. Acutely feeling the lack of a Nursing Home in his locality, he opened one in 1981 - AROGYA - which became part of the landscape of our childhood. A landmark. Located right on the main road, just a few yards from the Kankurgachi 'more', close to the 3A bus-stand. In fact, after graduating from Calcutta Medical College in 1999, and post his internship and house-staff-ship at his alma mater, it is in AROGYA that Saurabh invested the early years of his professional life. Unfortunately, things were not going too well after his father's death in 2001, and AROGYA had to be closed down in October 2007; a very painful moment for the family.

Saurabh had by then already joined KMC, and was married. His private practice, however, picked up a little later – after the birth of his son (his lucky charm)! And it has only strengthened ever since. But thankfully, he still has time for old patients!

S's SUMMER (23 June 2019)

S had a filmi summer. Five weeks of being mostly in Kolkata in this sweltering heat meant being indoors for at least half the day, most days. She did get to 'explore' her city a bit - Jorasanko Thakurbai, Birla Planetarium, Princep Ghat, Nehru Children's Museum (all of which will now be dutifully used in English compositions and Social Studies projects at school) - but the joy of those explorations fell short of the sheer relief of being in the cool of AC rooms. A sad reality!

A lot of those cool hours were spent watching films this summer: *Student of the Year* (SOTY) 2, *Durgeshgorer Guptodhon* (The Hidden Treasures of Durgeshgor, DG), and *Aladdin* in the theatres; and many more on her Mamma's laptop at home. I was not surprised at all that she liked *Aladdin*, but was taken aback by her responses to the other two: she called SOTY 'faltu' (I occasionally watch faltu stuff and do faltu things with her... it is good for the soul... but I had not expected her to spot it in a film so correctly); and she loved DG! Especially, the 'History Rap', and the graphics at the beginning and end of the film. She actually wanted to watch the film again! That did not happen, of course, but the songs from the film on YouTube (including a very devotional one) became a favourite pastime of hers for a while. She loves Ma Durga and Durga Puja.... her fascination for the mystery in the film and the songs have a lot to do with it, I guess. And I think Abir Chatterjee can safely add one more (little) fan to his growing list :)

The films that S watched at home were old favourites of mine, seen when I was her age, with my mother and sister: *Dadar Kirti* (which was the first film I ever saw as a child), *Balika Badhu (*the Hindi one starring Sachin and Rajni Sharma, featuring the lovely song 'bade achhe lagte hai'), *Kabuliwala* (with Chhabi Biswas in the title role), *Guddi*, *Parichay* (I have always been a Jaya Bhaduri fan) and *Pather Panchali* (on Vimeo, with Spanish subtitles!).

S had distinct responses to all these films: she loved the bond between the sisters in *Dadar Kirti*; the sarees and jewellery that *Balika Badhu* wore; she adored little Mini and her antics in *Kabuliwala*; liked Guddi's short frocks, long hair and big eyes with the kajal drawn out so; and she was bored stiff with the long back-stories of Jeetendra and Sanjeev Kumar's characters in *Parichay*, though she promptly took to the 'sa re ke sare' song with the children and asked me whether the teacher will marry the 'aunty' at the end!

I loved watching all these films with her – re-living, as I did, many precious moments of my childhood through them. But watching Satyajit Ray's *Pather Panchali* together was an altogether different experience: it was last week; she was pestering me for a film, she wanted to see *Frozen* again, but my Netflix account was not working... she was crestfallen... so I took a chance. I said I can show her a brother and sister story, which also had some cats and dogs in it. Would she be interested? "Yes", she said. And she was! She was completely drawn into the story; not for one moment did her interest flag. That was a revelation! I was actually quite prepared to hear that she is getting bored. She does not like black and white films, after all; she loves colour. Plus, there is pain and poverty in the film. I had no idea how she would react to them, though I was willing to guide her through the story. I decided I would stop if she wanted me to. But no – not only did she never ask me to stop, she was full of questions: "Why is the mother always angry?", "Why is the aunt SO old?", "Did Durga really steal the necklace of her friend?". And she simply loved Apu and Durga and her cats and dog, the reflection of the sweet-seller in the water, the train in the distant horizon with the children running through the kash fields, Durga getting drenched in the rain, swirling round and round with her long hair upturned. How stupid of me to think Srishti would be bored with *Pather Panchali*... this is a story about childhood. How can a child not respond to it?!

S loves to read story books, and there was that, too, of course, during the holidays – an Amar Chitra Katha *Shakuntala*, a recent graphic novel on Sita, a collection of *Fairy Tales* titled *5-minute Princess Stories* and a charming little book (a Dutch publication in English) called *The Girl in the Golden Dress*, featuring Rembrandt's famous painting, 'The Night Watch'. She pored over these books multiple times, reading them both with me and alone, and then making me repeat the stories to her at bedtime – all this, notwithstanding, this summer was definitely a summer of films! It was suitably capped with a visit to Ramoji Film City in Hyderabad, where her Jethu and Jethima (paternal uncle and his wife) live with their children. The children, H and J, are actually young adults now, but they have another furry sibling - Sid - who is S's favourite!

Just two days back, I asked her what she liked MOST about her summer holidays that were now coming to an end: without a moment's thought, she said, "playing with Sid"!

I have my own favourite moment from her summer: a particularly lazy morning sometime in early June. Thing is, on any given day, S spends a substantial part of her waking hours thinking of and impersonating animals (the more domesticated variety, I must add – cats, dogs, birds, rabbits, butterflies). But that morning was different: she saw a picture of a duck on the cover of an exercise book... and suddenly, longingly, remembered the ducks she would chat with every day, walking on her way to school and back. In the canals that lined our neighbourhood in Amsterdam. "If I go and visit them now, will they remember me?" she asked. Then, as a kind of ode to them, she sketched a duck in a pond and coloured it lovingly – that single activity taking up almost her entire morning. She loves animals. They are her best 'pretend' friends. I hope this imagination stays!

Ma on my Facebook Wall, in August (26 August 2019)

29 August 2014

My mother, the closet writer, has come out at last!

At 70, she has published her first book of fiction in Bangla – *Mukh-Michhil* (A Procession of Faces). It is a collection of 45 short stories (or 'anu-golpo', as they are called in Bangla). Initially inspired by the popular Bengali writer Banaphool's 'Natun Golpo' in the late 1970s, she has been writing off and on in this genre ever since.

Encouraged by her uncle, the well-known author Manoj Basu, Ma actually started writing in the 1960s - when she studied and taught Bengali literature - but except for some sporadic submissions in magazines, did not publish till recently. She has never stopped writing, though. She is blessed with an inexhaustible fount of creativity: gathering dust in her desk-drawers are hundreds of poems (poetry is her first love), also limericks, short stories and an unfinished novel! For many years now, I have been coaxing her to take them out, with my sister and father later joining the chorus. In 2010, a book of 'chhara' (rhymes) for children was published. *Mukh-Michhil* was about to come out soon after… but as often happens with books, it took a long time to find the right publisher.

Ma's life had begun with rainbow hues… and then after marriage… it became monochromatic for decades – a familiar enough tale, which she has herself turned extraordinary, by keeping her passion for writing alive through all the travails of her life. I only hope that the colour comes back to her life again, brightened anew by sharing her writing with the world!

So, here's introducing - with incredible joy and immense pride - my mother, the writer Kalpana Basu Roy.

24 August 2016

KALPANA BASU ROY (1944 – 2016) - Mother, teacher, friend, soul-mate.

Ma passed away most suddenly on 20 August, three days after suffering a massive cerebral stroke.

There was no chance to do anything…

She died as she had lived – without disturbing her daughters.

20 August 2019

It's been three years since Ma left us.

A part of me died with her. The rest of me... is hobbling along, battling all that life has to throw, without the balm of her tender presence, the weekly reassurance of her voice.

I never really got a chance to grieve her death. Yes, 'death'; I won't call it 'passing away' anymore. I doubt its meaning now. 'Passing away' into what? Another existence? – may be, I don't know. And I won't really know until I die. And then, it would be too late to argue with those living. I also refuse to call it 'passing away' because that sounds so much softer and does not do justice to the rude shock - and the finality - of what happened. 'Death' is far better, and the 'stop sound' of 'd' is phonetically, at least, a closer approximation of her ceasing to be.

After her death, I gave much thought to the meaning of the word 'death' – "the permanent ending of vital processes in a cell or tissue". Yes, it is an end – so please, let us call it that.

This definition of 'death' is especially brought home to a Hindu while undergoing the funeral rites. For there is something about witnessing a body you have loved (and being loved by) being reduced to a fistful of ashes that makes all grand philosophizing about death irrelevant. The putrid smell of burnt flesh that permeates a crematorium is also a memory that can never be completely erased from one's mind.

After death comes grief. That is a long road with an uncertain destination – depending, I believe, on what kind of relation you have had with the person dead. If it was vital, absolutely central to your identity, then you are just not mourning, but also undergoing a re-fashioning of identity, as *everything* has to be started anew, the world seen and felt through a permanent absence. No matter how mature you are in dealing with the fact of mortality, this re-fashioning is a slow and painful process, and one that just cannot be conveyed to those who have not known it.

I just called grief a long road – but it is not a linear track; rather, a circular loop of endlessly resuscitated memories. Some are poignant and nostalgic, that can be rationalized by a clearly discernible 'association of thought', and may elicit only a few silent tears or even a smile. Others are random moments from the past that often come flying at you without warning, and have the power to batter you down even as you seem to fare better with your sense of loss.

In these three years without Ma, I have managed to convince myself that it is a good thing that she is gone. The life she would have led after her severe cerebral attack, even if she came out of coma, would have been a cursed existence. What her life *could have been*, had she not had that attack, is a different matter... and actually a useless speculation. I have consciously avoided that path.

However, *what her life was*, as long as she had lived, is something that I have given a lot of thought. I have been moulded by her in a profound way... to an extent that it is at times difficult for me to understand what in me is truly mine and not just an extension of her. But in these three years of my mourning and re-fashioning of identity, I have critiqued her legacy and decided not to follow it blindly.

I want to emulate all that was life-affirming in Ma: her uncompromising honesty; her delight in the little things of life; her generosity towards others; her devotion to, and friendship with, us - her daughters; her ability to make literature (both in its cultivation and creation) sustain her. But I also choose to unfollow all that was persistently painful and disempowering in her life, which greatly limited the realms of the 'possible' for her, not allowing her to achieve what she eminently could or get what she richly deserved.

And the single most important thing in which I DON'T WANT to follow her is to die with my desk drawers full of incomplete manuscripts.

KAJAL DI (5 September 2019)

When I joined Presidency College in November 1992, as a student of English Honors, I had joined with my own baggage of historical knowledge about the institution. I knew all about the original Hindu College; of Derozio and his 'Young Bengal'; the 'stairway to heaven'; of Amartya Sen and Satyajit Ray and Aparna Sen; of the Naxal rebels of the 1970s, the 'gherao' of the principal and the standstill of the University. I knew all that! And of course, the 'tyesh' girls who famously smoke and drink.

But all that baggage melted away when I actually started studying there. For one, I myself overturned some of the stereotypes – because I did not smoke and drink. And I was not 'tyesh'. (Though I think I have always been smart and confident).

Every Department in Presidency had its own lore, and none more so than the English Department, which was one of the first to be established. Among our teachers, the senior most was Kajal di - Prof. Kajal Sengupta - who was already a living legend by then. She was the first female lecturer of the college: had joined it in 1958, at a time when there were no separate loos for women! She had done her graduation from Loreto College, went to Cambridge thereafter, and then came back and joined Presidency. We once saw a photograph of hers from that time. She was soooooo beautiful! One of our classmates, on seeing the photo, said: "I wish I had a time machine… could then go and meet this young Kajaldi". He voiced our collective sentiment!

Kajaldi had silky white hair, which she tied up in a bun. The red dot on her forehead was that of a lipstick; high-power spectacles covered her big eyes and sat steadily on her sharp nose. And if you saw her sideways, you then noticed the kajal that gave her her name – two short black lines of kohl coming outward from the rim of her eyes. She was short and slim, and carried loads of books to class, books that wobbled above and below the long attendance register we had. I had never seen her pin her sari. She wore only white; white saris with broad borders. They were never too bright, but did not lack colour either: she wore a range of sober, elegant colours and patterns; a lot of them *dure* – bangle lines, in contrasting colours.

She reminded me of my mother, who mostly wore Bengal cotton, *taat*, all her life– at home and outside; and her taste was very sober. Hence, in my mind, *taat* has always been associated with sobriety and elegance. And thriftiness, as Ma would never buy an expensive saree.

Kajaldi made a fashion statement out of white cottons. Sorry, style statement – fashions come and go, style remains. She wore the sari in the way I like best – with the *par* (border) covering her chest diagonally, and the *aanchal* left hanging as it should be.

In her introductory lecture on English Literature, I remember, she had talked of the woods and the trees: that we should be mindful of both. We should know the individual trees well, but never lose sight of the forest of which it is a part. The literary texts that we were taught were the trees, while History of English Literature (HEL) was the forest. She taught my favourite novelist (Thomas Hardy), Blake's poems, and the Renaissance, among other topics. But in the tutorial, we covered everything. How I waited for those tutorials the whole week! I got her as my tutor in the 3rd year, and I would like to believe that I had earned that, after doing well in Part-I. I still retain, and treasure, those tutorial exercise-books, with Kajaldi's comments in a sprawling handwriting, written all over: between the lines, along the margins, and on the left-hand side page, which was expressly kept blank for the purpose!

Kajaldi had married late. For a long time, she enjoyed life as a single, independent woman. She had a separate set of keys, she had told me once, and when she returned home late at night, while she unlocked the door with her own keys, she felt a delicious sense of freedom.

She did not have children, but brought up her nephew and niece as her own. And every year, for more than three decades, mothered a new batch of students in the English Department. As a teacher and tutor, she was without equal, and no one questioned or contested that in a Department where there was no dearth of talented teachers. Some of her younger colleagues were once her students – the brightest. So, the Department had a true 'parampara'.

What she meant to her students - several generations of them - became amply clear on the day of her memorial service at her home in February 2006. Scores of them came - from the relatively young to the very old - to pay their last respects to a teacher who epitomized intellectual rigor and honesty and who taught both passionately and well. I remember sitting among them, feeling completely at one with them, shedding silent tears.

She is one of the best teachers that I have had the privilege of being taught by, and I was lucky to continue to receive her affection long after I ceased to be a student. As a teacher and a human being, she has left an indelible mark on me. I still dream of her!

NO 'NARI SHAKTI' PLEASE! (20 September 2019)

Ma Durga is coming to town… how do you know? You have hoardings everywhere of Sourav Ganguly sharing banner space with the latest Tollywood beauties (read MPs) who (try to) impersonate a raging Durga about to slay the demon Mahishashur. The latter, however, for reasons of space, could not be accommodated in the banner. I found that symbolic. For the real demon that the Durgas of the world have to continually contend with - patriarchy - is an invisible force, insidiously and relentlessly powerful, and still very far from being slain!

Hence, I am a little sick of the annual reminders of 'nari shakti' (female power) every time Ma Durga visits us: of how, like Durga, we women are the very embodiment of 'shakti', naturally multitasking with our invisible ten hands; and though we are full of the milk of human kindness, we have our 'rudra' side, too. Hence… men, beware! Do not cross your line!

Make no mistake: I have no doubts about women being multitaskers or having huge reserves of inner strength. I do not doubt because I have those qualities myself; I belong to the tribe, after all. My question is: what really constitutes 'shakti'? And what exactly are we celebrating? Shakti means both strength and power. We have strength – but not power. Sorry!

All around me, I see women with immense strength – mostly, the strength to endure, which has been the badge of our tribe for millennia. But there is also the determination to fight adversity, the willingness to be patient with life and people. Endurance, patience, fortitude – these are not just adjectives in the lives of women; they are lived realities, far more than they are with men. (Multiply the need for those qualities manifold in the case of lower-class/caste women). And then there is the enormous responsibility of bringing up children, the onus of which is still, overwhelmingly, on women. As are homemaking and caregiving, in general.

I do not see any radical shift in gender roles in our society. There are more women with degrees now, yes; also, more women who earn their living. But that does not necessarily translate into empowerment. For many, it actually leads to double enslavement – at home and in the workplace. Money can give financial independence – but true empowerment is a different thing. It is the ability to define the terms of one's own existence, unapologetically; to stand up for one's rights and stand by one's principles, without compromise; and, very importantly, to enable others to do the same. Very few among us can do that.

So, during Durg Puja, let us wear our new sarees and shoes and jewellery, do *pandal*-hopping with our friends, participate in *anjali* with our families, enjoy the rhythm of the *dhaak* and *dhunuchi*, gorge on delicious food... but PLEASE, let us not talk about 'nari shakti'!

Durga Puja in Kolkata (26 September 2019)

It is that time of the year again – when Ma Durga comes visiting with her four children (Lakshmi, Saraswati, Ganesh and Kartik) to her natal home down in the plains, leaving her husband's (Lord Shiva) abode in the Himalayas for ten days. Bengalis celebrate it unfailingly wherever in the world they may be. However, nothing can match the native celebration in Bengal, especially in the city of Kolkata.

This will be my third Durga Puja in Kolkata after leaving the Netherlands in 2017. For a decade before that, I was always away during this time, visiting the city annually only in Christmas.

The Expat Experience

Honestly speaking, I did not exactly miss Durga Puja in the Netherlands. As part of KALLOL, the Indian Bengali Association there, we celebrated it with much fanfare at Voorschoten every year; and actually, did it in a way and with an involvement that we had never done in Kolkata. But the expat experience is very different; both less and more 'authentic' than the real one. More, because in its eagerness, it often goes overboard in observing the rituals; and less, because it can never approximate the experience of the city.

Back in Kolkata

For the ten days of the Puja, Kolkata is transformed… the whole city is decked as a bride and looks beautiful! I witnessed this after ages in 2017 and 2018. My predilection was actually to sleep through it - the previous two months in both years having been exceptionally exhausting for me - but my daughter, S, was super-enthusiastic about the Pujas and I could not deny her that. Especially, in the first year, as it took her mind away from missing Amsterdam. By the second Durga Puja in October 2018, however, she was already enjoying the Puja for its own sake.

Incidentally, what she loves most about it - the lights in the streets - is neither very uniquely Indian nor Bengali. The big capitals of the West are as resplendent with light during Christmas. And for a longer time. The festive mood always prolonged a tad bit (I feel). What is unique about the Durga Puja, however, is the 'pandals' - or pavilions - where the goddess is housed with her family.

'Pandal-hopping' during the Pujas is an inevitable part of a Bengali's (actually anyone's) childhood in Kolkata. I have had my fair share of it as a child and teenager, but had long stopped enjoying that bit later. Because, over the years, I felt the core of the festival had been overshadowed by the frills. The *puja* itself - the worship of the goddess, the prayer part - had been pushed into the background; and what became increasingly important was the scale and grandeur of the pavilions. And I hated the gendered long queues before all the reputed pandals, having to spend hours to see just one idol. What an utter waste of time! I much preferred spending the puja days with my two bosom pals at each other's homes, wearing new sarees of course (that part I have always loved), and content with admiring each other!

In 2017, I did not mind the usual Puja stuff so much as I was seeing everything afresh through S's eyes, and because we did very low-key pandal-hopping, restricting ourselves to our neighbourhood (with no queues), and a spin through (part of) North Kolkata in our car one evening. But last year, S got a real taste of the excitement of pandal-hopping when she saw one of the most famed and expensive pandals (with its idols decked in gold) at Sreebhumi. She also enjoyed her time with the children of two of my friends who are roughly the same age as her, the meetings allowing inter-generational friendships that added a totally new dimension to our socializing!

The 'para'

Throughout the Pujas in the last two years, in the midst of all the renewed excitement imparted by my daughter, I was reminded a lot of one of my conversations about vanishing neighbourhoods in Asian cities with Prof. Mike Douglass, a social scientist renowned for his work on urban planning in Asia (in an interview that I had taken of him at IIAS, Leiden, in June 2016). Because if the Durga Puja is anything, it is one great valorisation of the neighbourhood – the 'para', as we call it in Bangla. For the ten days of the festival, one's identity is principally tied to one's 'para', and there is *fierce* competition regarding the pandals. Especially after Asian Paints instituted an award for the best pandal in the 1990s. 'Durga Puja Committees' in hundreds of paras have vied with each other ever since to rope in the best idol-makers, artists and architects in a bid to win the prize. There is tremendous creativity that this months' long effort and enthusiasm engenders. I admire that enthusiasm – though never unreservedly.

The unsavoury bit

Let me share an anecdote to explain why: On the last working day before the Pujas in 2017, I was late in returning home. On my way back from College Street, the only cab driver who agreed to take me home decided to go for a shortcut – just before Manicktola, to avoid the inevitable longer waits at the main signals on that route during this festive season. But it turned out to be not so much a shortcut of distance as a shortcut to darkness. Within a few seconds, from blinding lights, we were literally plunged into total darkness: a stinking, suffocating darkness, where ghost-like figures in hovels went about resignedly with a cursed existence.

It is such a cliché to talk of the disparities between the rich and the poor in the metros in India (as in most megacities in the world). We in Kolkata are used to seeing slums along the road; people washing, cleaning, bathing openly, displaying an almost cheerful kind of street domesticity. But the experience of that pre-puja evening was very different: it brought home to me the fact that all those glittering lights on the main streets in long preparation for festivities to come must necessarily exclude the poor, especially the abysmally poor.

It is this disparity that I have found the most difficult to accept after my return, post my ten years in the Netherlands. I had lived in Kolkata for 33 years before that. So, the differences of caste and class are not new to me. And yet, the utter disparity between the haves and have-nots now strikes me in a way that it did not before. Not even during our mandatory, annual three-week holidays. Have I changed? Or has the city become more unequal? I do not know.

'Pujo-pujo rob'

Durga Puja is in the air. The seasonal markers of 'sarat' - when the Puja happens - are unmistakable: 'shoroter megh, kaash phool' (the clouds of sarat, kaash flowers) ....

Kolkata dwellers do not get to see much of that, though. But there are other unavoidable signifiers: for one, there are the innumerable hoardings for Puja shopping everywhere, with all brands advertising their 'special Puja collection' and all products offering a 'special Puja discount', of course. Not to speak of all female models (read Tollywood, and of late Bollywood, heroines) wearing the traditional Bengali red-bordered white sari to endorse everything from jewellery and clothes to turmeric and cooking oil.

But increasingly, as the Puja days approach, the most visible sign of its countdown is the work-in-progress 'pandals' that come up everywhere – that not only restrict the traffic flow at several important junctions of the city, but also necessitate all kinds of commuting re-arrangements within neighbourhoods. The resulting inconvenience is usually borne willingly by the residents!

The ten days of the Puja - with the festivities rising to a crescendo in the last four days - can easily be termed as one of the greatest shows on earth: it definitely rivals the biggest cultural festivals anywhere in the world. But on the tenth and last day - 'Dashami'

- the gregariousness of the celebrations is toned down by the poignancy of the goddess's return to her husband, leaving her natal home. In a culture where a woman's identity is still overwhelmingly tied up with her marital status, Durga's return has an emotional resonance that few other pujas have in India.

But then, Bengalis look forward to the next year saying, 'Ascchhe bochhhor abar hobe', even as they immerse the goddess in the Ganges.

EXPERIENCING PAIN AT SEVEN (11 November 2019)

S was very sad today. Her first best friend broke up with her second-best friend in school. She tried to patch up the 'brokening'. It did not work.

At first, I tried to soften her sadness by jokingly asking whether it was like Peppa pig breaking up with Suzzy sheep (in a favourite episode from her favourite cartoon) and then coming together again at the slightest opportunity (only to fight again...)! But no, this was serious.

In her recounting, I realized that she is herself the second-best friend of her first best friend (did not know that). I asked her whether that hurt her. She said, no: she was more hurt by the other pair not being friends anymore. She in fact, had even reasoned with her first best friend that the one she is leaving had come into her life before (in Upper Nursery) while S had become her friend only in Grade 1. That reasoning did not work either.

I was stumped hearing this part. In her own way, in her language, S was talking of primary loyalties, of fidelity in friendships. Her sense of fairness was hurt: she felt the person who came first in her first best friend's life should have the greater claim in their inter-personal relationship.

I could not make out what had affected S more – that her two friends breaking up tarnished the happy dynamic of their triad, or (what she thought was) the unfairness of her remaining the friend and the older pair not.

She asked me about my school friends... I think she needed to validate her experience by relating it to mine. I readily obliged. Told her of my friends – those who have stayed and the ones I lost. Told her, too, of the importance of togetherness in building and keeping friendships; that there can be other ways of not being friends any more than quarrelling or falling out. She was quick to understand the logic of outgrown friendships, immediately citing a friend from Grade 1 who is not a close friend of hers anymore in Grade 2, as she is now in a different section and they hardly get to do anything together. I marvelled at this understanding.

In all probability, the triad that S loves being a part of will be restored soon (in which case, they will insist that their mothers plan play dates even before the winter break). But that does not alter the fact that the sadness she felt today was very real.

We try to protect our children from pain – but they get it anyway. And we sure underestimate their maturity. These are the two lessons I learnt today.

BROTOTI (5 December 2019)

Last Friday, I took S to the annual function of 'Choopkatha' at the Rabindra Okakura Bhavan, Salt Lake. Helmed by veteran theatre artist, Dolly Basu, 'Choopkatha' is a theatre group that works with differently-abled children – using this art form as a means to develop their communication and confidence. The group also includes other children in their programs and the kids all get to perform together in the annual show. This year, they did a medley of items – children's nursery rhymes, Sukumar Ray's *Ha Ja Ba Ra La*, a recitation of Tagore's poem 'Puraton Bhritya', and a dramatization of Richard Bach's *Jonathan Livingstone Seagull*. The children performed very well and deservedly got a thunderous applause from the audience. At the end, Dolly Basu acknowledged the parents, without whose support and participation, the program would not have been possible. Among those mentioned was the compere of the evening, Brototi Dasgupta – one of my dearest friends.

Brototi's son, Sunny, played the role of 'hijibijbij' in *Ha Ja Ba Ra La*. This is his third annual performance with 'Choopkatha', and he has enjoyed it more every year. He is very active in sports at his school, La Martiniere for Boys, especially in football, and goes for private coaching in the game twice a week. He revels in this physical exercise. But Brototi is all for the development of a well-rounded personality, and has thus encouraged Sunny to take up chess (in which he already excels) and pursue something creative as well. For the latter, she first tried a two-year customized course in music (aimed at four- to six-year-olds) at the Calcutta School of Music, but it did not go down well with him. 'Choopkatha', however, has been more rewarding: theatre definitely suits him better, and he has also learnt to be more sympathetic, Brototi tells me, through his interactions with differently-abled children.

This is a new phase in our relationship: this sharing of the experience of motherhood – what our children are doing in school, their interests and passions, the ever-new things in their lives. It lends a whole new dimension to a long friendship.

✦✦✦

Brototi was first a colleague of mine who soon became a friend and a sister. Just two years younger than me, she has always given me the respect due to an elder sister - a 'didi' - in our society, even as she shared her most intimate thoughts and feelings uninhibitedly with me, like friends/equals do. It is a subtle balance that she has effortlessly managed to maintain for seventeen years now.

Subtlety is indeed her hallmark – subtlety of thought, of expression. Her other distinguishing characteristic is her depth of feeling. I honestly know very few people who have the emotional depth she has. It stems from her love of literature, no doubt, but also music. She had trained in Rabindrasangeet from the famed music academy, 'Dakshinee', and till date, continues to learn it from her beloved former teacher, Sumita Ghosh. But there is also another crucial factor at play here: a spiritual core in her that is averse to anything remotely shallow in word or deed, which compels her to continually see things beneath the skin. She also has this marvellous ability to make the songs she learns/sings touchstones by which to live. In fact, it is this love of song, especially Rabindrasangeet, which has been a special bond between us: we have a secret code of certain songs that are pathways to our pasts, to specific days and special moments we have shared, to our unique joys and sorrows.

When I first met Brototi in 2002 as a tenured faculty member at Basantidevi College (BDC), I was struck by her beauty: sharp features, curly hair, glowing skin and a slim figure somehow added up to that elusive thing we call 'labonya' in Bengali. There was also the faint aura of her family background about her, which she was quick to dismiss whenever asked. She was the granddaughter of legendary scholar Subodh Chandra Sengupta, whose books on Shakespeare we mandatorily read during our university years. (I had found his edition of *Macbeth*, in particular, invaluable during my Part II Hons).

Brototi lived up to her family name, topping in English Honours at Lady Brabourne in her year and securing a first-class second in her M.Phil at Calcutta University. When she taught at BDC, she taught part-time in a number of other colleges/institutes as well – Muralidhar Girls College, Vivekananda College for Women and the RKM Institute of Languages. Additionally, she also gave private tuitions to college students at home.

She was just not busy at that time, but maniacally so. I had found in her routine a determination to leave no hour, no 'bela' empty. I had felt as if she was killing time, killing her weeks rather than living them. Immersing herself in so much teaching that there was no energy left to think at all. Either she wanted to forget something or was running away from something, I had thought.

There could of course be the other possibility – of the desperate need to earn as much money as possible through part-time work to support her family while waiting for a full-time job. But visits to her Ekdalia home and meeting her parents made me realize that that was not the case. Her geologist father had by then comfortably retired from the Central Fuel Research Institute and the family had settled down in their ancestral home in Kolkata, after spending most of Brototi's (and her elder brother's) growing-up years in undivided Bihar (Ranchi, Dhanbad) and Assam (Jorhat).

She was at BDC for only two years. But what a great time we had! We actually interacted more outside the college than within its premises, spending a lot of time in and around Gariahat – walking back together from college to the Ekdalia auto stand (this was the mainstay of our friendship), shopping in Pantaloons, buying other sundry stuff from pavement hawkers, eating out, watching a film or two. Being with her was always a joy, but some days stand out – a Saraswati Puja spent together, a long relaxed (what we call our) "macaroni and cheese afternoon" at my home during a summer break, my Birthday in 2004, 'Shasti' of the same year… She actually remembers the details much more than I do, startling me sometimes with the memory of things I had said or done and what they had meant to her.

✦✦✦

She married in January 2005. And then went to live in Bangalore, the city her husband, Debanjan - an electrical engineer trained at JU and IIT Delhi - had made his own since 1996. She started teaching full-time at Mount Carmel soon after relocating to Bangalore and led a very happy life there for a couple of years. I was a witness to it in October 2005, when, while staying with my sister (who also worked there) for a week, I visited Brototi's home. On a rain-drenched day. The idea was to spend only the evening. But massive showers ensured that I stayed the night with the newly married couple. I remember how the very air of their home was imbued with the romance of new domesticity: the working couple returning home and sharing their day over coffee, the husband busy stocking up the fridge with provisions, the wife lovingly cooking 'bhoonyi khichri' (with an assortment of items to go with it). On the face of it, nothing different from any other working couple… just the way they went about it, which made it clear that the ritual was still new.

The next morning saw Brototi laying out an elaborate breakfast – complete with protein, carbohydrate, calcium and fibre. I marvelled at the meticulousness with which she ensured the complete diet.

I was also impressed by another thing: Debanjan's choice collection of books and CDs, probably because I have known few in his profession with such a literary/aesthetic bent of mind. I remember taking *The Book of Laughter and Forgetting* with me to bed that night.

After Bangalore, the couple had shifted to Delhi in 2009 and were blessed with a son the year after. Brototi was then teaching at Amity, Noida, but gave up her job during her pregnancy. She never returned to work thereafter. It was a conscious decision on her part, driven in equal measure by a desire to devote herself full time to raising a child (inspired in this by a friend of hers) and also by the reality of her domestic situation – the fact that she knew she would not be able to avail the kind of family support that working mothers need to sustain their careers.

✦✦✦

I never had the chance to visit her Delhi home. After 2005, I met her only in December 2012. By then, they had relocated to Kolkata. A lot had happened in our lives in the intervening seven years, motherhood being the most recent and overwhelming of our experiences. I refused to eat anything that December afternoon at her home, lest we have less time to talk. There was so much to say, to share. I settled instead for four rounds of Darjeeling tea and two packs of 'Nice' biscuits!

Her new - and permanent - home in New Town is a delight: aesthetically done, with enormous thought given to the littlest of things. To be with her is a great way to unwind - her home's cozy interior, her hospitality, and the quiet of her surroundings make it the ideal getaway for me for a few hours. Only, I have not had much scope to enjoy that getaway.

She is one of the few people in Kolkata who insist on meeting at home and cooking a meal for me. No matter how hard I try to dissuade her from it, always pleading for uncluttered conversation (as the socializing time at my disposal is invariably short), she adamantly sticks to her guns: "Of course, Ritu di, we will talk. We will eat and talk". I enjoy whatever she cooks, but more than that, I feel grateful for what she so generously offers (despite my protestations). With my mother and an entire generation of aunts - not to speak of grandmothers - passing away, there are few left to feed me. And here she is, a younger sister and friend, taking on that role on her own!

We had spent only a very short time together as departmental colleagues. Most of the rest of the fifteen years have been spent cherishing the memory of that time! Seven years without seeing each other, and then, on average, meeting up once a year. This was the case not only from 2012 to 2016 (while I was still in the Netherlands and visited Kolkata annually), but it is true even after my return in 2017. I earnestly hope we can meet more frequently in the coming years.

COPING WITH COVID (2020–2021)

MY FIRST TWO READERS (19 Jan 2020)

Sunday morning in Kolkata. Here are two of my first readers, reading GARIAHAT JUNCTION while basking in the winter sun.

Reader 1: An 84-year-old ex-professor of Physics, his monkey cap marking him out as a Bengali as nothing else can (in winter)! He had read an incomplete draft years ago and is relishing re-visiting the collection (with a magnifying glass), one story at a time. (In my mind's eye, I imagine his absent wife sitting beside him, fighting with him to read the book first...)

Reader 2: A seven-year-old dreamy creature, whose days (outside of school) are mostly spent in talking to her 'pretend' friends. She was *furious* to know that this is not a 'children's book'. And it did not placate her one bit when I told her that the book is dedicated to her. I further tried mollifying her by saying, "OK, I will read out portions from it to you. Happy"? "No", came the defiant reply. "I will read it myself, whether I understand it or not"!

That is precisely what she has been doing since yesterday. Stuck in a traffic jam in Gariahat Junction, while returning from her ballet class with her dad, she called me up to say that she is reading GARIAHAT JUNCTION at Gariahat Junction! And then, very helpfully, suggested: "You know, I can give you an idea... you can write a story about me stuck in this jam, reading your book".

It melts my heart to see my child wanting desperately to enter my imaginary world. But she has also, in the same breath, made me feel hopelessly inadequate as a writer. "When will you write a children's book?" she had asked me; it was not so much an irritated question as a challenge! I am not sure I am up to taking it up... for I simply do not have the imagination of her 'dida' (my mother), who could flit between poetry and prose, writing for adults and children with effortless ease.

And as she determinedly continues to read my book, I have another worry – that she will chance upon the 'adult' bits much before she is supposed to...!

ICU STEPDOWN (17 March 2020)

"Time is in slow motion here. Every painful minute dragged out in 60 slow seconds. Every 30 minutes an eon, every hour an eternity.

They are all laid out in rows – old, shrunk bodies, their life drawn out of them, almost sucked dry… The first night that Baba was admitted to this 'ICU Stepdown', it was such a ghastly sight! Seeing those rows of shrouded bodies, all with their eyes closed… made it seem like purgatory...

I was reminded of Ma just eighteen months back – in the third and final day of her coma, her face distorted, her belly bloated, her entire left side stiff as stone after the cerebral attack... a misshapen body that was once a mother. She, too, was sleeping in the midst of such rows of bodies on either side. Thankfully, her stay was short in that purgatory…

Already, in this one week here, some patients have gone… who knows where? … and I see new faces in their stead. I remember two people whom I cannot see anymore: there was this woman, who looked so ancient it was a miracle she was alive at all. She was visited in the mornings by a son who was very old himself. Another patient made painful sounds at night (that disturbed Baba no end), but fared better in the mornings. Later in the week, I actually saw him in a different part of the room, much recovered. Even in sleep, he had looked imposing. Must have been someone everyone revered, or perhaps, was downright afraid of. He was tall, and when awake, spoke with a raspy voice. He had a hurt expression on his face that seemed to say: "How can life do this to me? This is not me!"

The others in the room are way beyond such emotions. They have no energy, no feelings, nothing left. They are just aware of the discomfort of their bodies… they just want to sleep sweet sleep.

*****

I wrote the above bit in mid-February 2018, on my newly gifted mobile, while waiting to see Baba during 'visiting hours'. He had fallen asleep, I was told, just before I came in at 11 am to meet him. I did not want to disturb him… so I just waited… and while I waited and looked around me, to the other patients in that room, I typed on my Samsung 'Notes', to keep my mind from straying into dark thoughts. Darker, that is, than what I was recording.

Baba had had a freak kidney failure a week before, suddenly one night, and was admitted to that facility within a few hours. Twelve days later, he was shifted to one of the biggest private hospitals in the city, where he stayed for another three weeks. Most of that time was spent in the ICU. At one point, the doctors seemed to run out of options... and then, miraculously… he recovered. He was bedridden for a few months upon returning home, but back on his feet thereafter, though still confined at home.

He is now as normal as we can hope him to be at 84. I have not seen a more disciplined octogenarian. He follows his daily routine with clockwork precision: from meals to taking medicine (which is a lot), from doing his rudimentary exercise to reading newspaper headlines with a magnifying glass in the sun and watching a particular Bengali soap every evening (this last surprises me no end, given his lifelong disinterest in TV). I have also not seen a busier man – he can somehow spend the whole day just being preoccupied with himself! He even seldom talks over the phone with the few younger friends (his peers have all died) and the one sibling he is left with.

Part of the reason that the whole day is gobbled up just doing necessary things is that his body has slowed down. Whatever he does, he does at a much slower pace than before. Hence, the littlest of things take the longest time. He is a stoic and has always accepted life's realities without any complaints. But there are certain things he misses, the small joys of life… like making tea. He would not even trust Ma with that (after his retirement, i.e.). Now, on the rare occasions that he makes it, he feels utterly exhausted by the task. But he does not enjoy the tea that is served to him twice a day, either. None can do it exactly right. He has always been a great connoisseur of (Bengali) food; the kind who would discuss dinner while having lunch, and that very 'Bong' variety whose chief duty as householder was to do the 'bajar' (grocery), so that he could get just the things he wanted. Given this history, the many dietary restrictions that his medical condition has imposed upon him were not easy for him to take. But I feel it is the tea that bothers him more. Life's beauty, for him, has gone down yet another notch because of it. *That* is a 'stepdown'.

Life in general, for an octogenarian, is a step down. Is it not?

I MUST add here, though, that till 82, till that freak kidney failure two years back, Baba defied every stereotype of old age, with his enviable energy and self-sufficiency. Now, however, he is like most others his age. He is an old man!

Since, for the longest time, he did not behave like one, I have had great difficulty in accepting his current condition. Especially, the physical part: he is thin as a stick, with hollow cheeks, shrunken eyes, near toothless gums, and a totally bald head (that for most of his life was only half bald). He is a shadow of himself…

And yet, and still… he remains my rock…!

WHEN HOME IS NOT HOME (23 March 2020)

In economic terms, COVID-19 has hit the daily wage labourer the most. Concerned citizens have many legitimate questions: What will happen to their wages during the shutdown? Those who work as domestic staff may still get paid leave, but what about those on the street? How will they survive?

For the general population above (or way above) the poverty line, the general consensus seems to be that the most positive way to look at the quarantine is to use/utilize/enjoy the time that has come unasked for – despite the many inconveniences.

I would like to add an invisible category to the list – the unfortunate ones for whom home is not what it is meant to be.

One would be surprised to know - or acknowledge - how many there are in this category. Like closet homosexuals, they are the closet homeless. They have a roof over their heads, no doubt - and let us be very clear about the privilege of having one - but the roof only covers the head. It cannot give security or warmth or a sense of belonging. No corner of it can truly be claimed as one's own; a place that one doesn't want to return to on weekdays and doesn't want to stay in on weekends.

During this quarantined period, my heart goes out to:

- Children, unloved and alienated at home, for whom school is the real home, and friends the only family;
- Youngsters for whom campus life means everything;
- Couples who live wholly separate lives while staying together, and for whom even weekends are a nightmare;

- Men and women who go out to work not only to earn a living but to breathe more freely outside the claustrophobic restrictions of their home;
- Homemakers who savour a small window of 'me-time' during the day when the household chores are done and the children/ spouse are yet to return;
- The elderly, who often feel out of place everywhere, both at home and outside; but, when at home, prefer a quiet home infinitely more to a noisy one; (Contrary to popular notion, loneliness is not what bothers them the most - they learn to get used to it sooner or later, some better than others - but the disruption in their routine. They just want peace, and a quarantined household, especially with children in it, cannot give them that.)
- The truly miserable: those who hate both their home and workplace, but in normal circumstances, can at least look upon one as a temporary respite from the other. They will now be denied that oscillation.

I am sure I have missed out some. But even in the case of those, my point remains the same: for far too many people, the outside world makes life at home bearable.

I sincerely hope they have the patience to bear this out...!

Home-quarantine: Through the Eyes of a 7-year-old (26 March 2020)

When she went to her weekly ballet class on Saturday, 14th March, S had no idea that her normal school routine was about to change drastically. On Saturday, 15th March, the West Bengal State Government declared suspension of all classes and exams in all educational institutions of the state till 31st March – to combat the spread of the COVID-19 virus. I broke the news to S only on Sunday night. She gave me a quizzical look… but thankfully was very sleepy and did not proceed to ask any questions.

Just a day later, the suspension was extended to 15th April. The whole of that week, her international school and the private undergraduate college where I teach, like all other educational institutions, were frantically trying to re-adjust to the new reality – working out the modalities of conducting online classes and working/learning from home. I was caught up in it both as parent and teacher, wondering whether this session/semester could get back on the normal track at all. Towards the end of the week, a 'janta' curfew was declared on Sunday, 22nd March. No sooner was it over than we came to know that there would be a 'lockdown' from Monday evening to Friday. But just a day later, Prime Minister Narendra Modi addressed the nation, declaring the extension of the lockdown till 15 April. In 10 days - from 14th to 24th March, to be precise - the enormity of the crisis was brought home to Indians, many of whom had deluded themselves into thinking that they were immune from such a calamity. My life, like everyone else's, has been vastly affected by this lockdown. Working from home, with a child and elderly parent, and in the absence of all domestic help, is a challenge that I am still in the process of figuring out how best to handle. But as the situation turned from bad to worse, and a looming threat morphed into an unprecedented crisis, it is my daughter's response to it that I tracked carefully – half-amazed/half-amused.

Here is her journey.

Monday, 16 March 2020 - Day 1:

"Mama, can we visit D and A, and will they come here during these 15 days? We'll have such FUN!"

I tell her that that's precisely what we *cannot* do: what is keeping her from school is also what will not allow her to visit her friends. She is crestfallen. Tears well up in her eyes immediately. A big tight hug and a bit of cooing about video-chats save the day.

Tuesday, 17 March 2020 - Day 2:

I make her a homeschool routine. She is super-duper excited. Like me, she *loves* planning! And very helpfully suggests:

"Mamma, you also make a routine for yourself, ok? We will work together. It will be such FUN!"

I love it when she says that, the *way* she says that - "such FUN" - with the involuntary stress on "FUN"; her eyes closed, her small palms joining in a joyous clap. Her ability to be happy with the littlest of things is a daily reminder for me of the innocence of childhood. She is actually in the habit of saying "It'll be such FUN!" for a wide variety of reasons – but I am floored whenever she includes an activity with me in that list!

Wednesday, 18 March 2020 - Day 3:

This is a day of reckoning. Her life has gone for a toss by an invisible enemy, and she deals with it fair and square in her English 'composition' of the day:

"My school is closed because of cronona varies.

I am not getting close to anyone because of that too.

I have been asked to wash my hands every hour.

I am not touching anyone because they have an infection and I don't want to spread it, that's why.

Mama has made a small rooteen for me and I am trying to follow that.

And now I am stuck with mama in the house. (Evidently, she is *not* having fun with me!)

I am staying away from meet and fish.

I am not going to any place and I am not going anywhere outside".

Thursday, 19 March 2020 - Day 4:

There is an accidental pink coordination in her outfit after her bath. And she also chanced upon her misplaced pink sunglasses the same afternoon. What do you think happens?

"Mama", I hear, while working on something (cannot recall what). I look up: there she is, giving me a pose. (She can pose anytime, anywhere)! We have a small photo session.

<u>Friday, 20 March 2020 - Day 5</u>:

She is furious with me:

"The whole day you are saying: "Don't do this", "Don't do that", "Don't touch this", "Don't kiss", "Don't put your hand inside your mouth", "Don't rub your eyes"...

She continues with some gibberish, and then... makes faces at me. I am appalled. But before I can respond to that verbally, she storms out of the bedroom.

"WE HAVE TO BE CAREFUL, beta", I shout back, helplessly....

<u>Saturday, 21 March 2020 - Day 6</u>:

Her dad had gifted her a portable chessboard, which he had ordered online. She had learnt the preliminaries of the game from him with great interest. But this evening, while playing by herself, she seems far more intrigued with the mechanism of the item: the wooden square board folds into a rectangular box, with all the combatants encased in a green velvet cushion inside. She opens the box into a board and shuts it back again into a box, innumerable times, taking out and putting back the double kings and queens, bishops and knights, and the rest of the gang. She gives them the freedom of movement that she is being denied.

<u>Sunday, 22 March 2020 - Day 7</u>:

S is in a lazy mood in the morning. That does not change much in the afternoon, but at some point, she plonks herself down on the sofa and making a table of her upraised knees, draws a set of flowers and a ballerina. I am surprised to see the firm breasts and cleavage of the ballerina (never mind her face and palms); but I love the flowers, especially the rose. The orange tinge on the left petal and the yellow tint on the left leaf are "because of the sunlight falling on it", she tells me. Her drawing teacher has taught her that, I'm informed. Her own favourite is the other (undefined) flower: she is mightily impressed with herself, with the shading she has been able to accomplish with her colour pencils. "Just pencils", she adds, in case I have missed the point.

Monday, 23 March 2020 - Day 8:

It has been exactly a week that she has been at home, and she is bored to death. I know it when she is pissed off with, of all things, PEPPA PIG! She is supposed to have outgrown Peppa a long time back. But she loves watching the series, and by now, probably knows all the dialogues of all the episodes by heart. I frequently see her mouthing the dialogues of Peppa or George or Suzy Sheep or Rebecca Rabbit while having her dinner – finishing a sentence someone has just begun or giving a response before it comes. And I see her laughing at the end of every episode with Peppa and her family, their backs to the ground and bellies thrust up.

But tonight she hungers for something new: "Why do they show the SAME episodes over and over again?

I am genuinely surprised. But I also know that a lot will happen in the next few hours. Getting bored can be very productive: S is at her creative best during these spells.

So first: she transformed herself into a fairy; and then, late at night, when her sleep just won't come (because, uncharacteristically, she has slept during the day), I ask her to style my hair. I need to write… and there is no other way of engaging her while I do so. Immediately, she is all fired up: with her small arsenal of clips and bands, she gets down to being the hairstylist, expertly commenting on the quality of my hair, of the need to oil it regularly, how the styling could have been so much better if it was longer, etc., etc…

Tuesday, 24 March 2020 - Day 9:

The happy effect of the hairstyling wears off with sleep. She wakes up with a rage and writes an angry letter to Corona Virus.

"Dear Corona Virus,

I would like you to get out of earth and travel to Mars, it's lovely there, nobody is there, and nobody will try to harm you. If you stay here, I will beat you! And squish you and kill you. If you don't want that to happen, then you better get lost from here.

Angry regards from Srishti".

*****

The PM will address the nation at 8 pm, we are told, the whole day long. S listens to the address in Hindi. I translate it for her in Benglish (Bengali + English). The PM is earnestly requesting the citizens to draw a 'Laxmanrekha' around their homes, and warning them of the dire consequences that will follow if they don't.

S knows the story of the *Ramayana* and understands the significance of the epic reference. She is quiet for a while and huddles close to me. After a long lovey-dovey session, I connect her to a friend of hers. They video-chat for a whole hour: she looks and sounds the happiest in 9 days! I have never been more grateful to WhatsApp than I was that night.

Wednesday, 25 March 2020 - Day 10:

I tell her I will be writing a post about her quarantine. She is delighted! As I select the photos and list down her activities of the last 10 days, date-wise, in preparation for the post, she sits by me and directs the photo edits.

"I love to see you write, Mamma", she tells me, before drifting off to sleep. And I melt!

While I write the post, she turns 180 degrees in bed and is now sprawled out diagonally across it, in magnificent abandon. Time for me to join her!

EXHAUSTED (3 April 2020)

There is only one word to sum up my experience of the last two weeks at home: exhausted!

The official 'lockdown' in India started a week after our educational institutions closed in West Bengal, including my college and my daughter's school. In the first week, we were thinking only in terms of a fortnight's disruption. So, that week of mine was mostly spent strategizing online teaching with my colleagues and settling my daughter down with a homeschool routine. These were re-adjustments for sure, but pretty manageable (even with the extra spring cleaning of the house that I undertook, as an exaggerated safety measure).

The principal fear of the first week for me was that I had the two most vulnerable categories for COVID-19 at home – below 10 (my daughter is almost 8) and above 60 (my dad is 84). But I was able to contain it, getting busy as I did with my new home schedule. The lockdown from 23rd March, however, changed the whole scenario drastically. For it meant a lockdown of goods and services. And the clamping of services is what affected me the most, as it meant that our domestic staff, most of whom commute by train from the suburbs, could not come anymore.

We have the standard domestic staff of any Indian household - especially with a working woman in it - the domestic help and cook. But since mine also includes both a child and an elderly person needing special care, we have a nanny and a night nurse as well. Now, I had to stand in single-handedly for all of them.

Replacing the nanny was the easiest part. My daughter is pretty self-sufficient, and I enjoy nothing more than spending time with her at home. That enjoyment is somewhat compromised, no doubt, when one is 'working from home', as opposed to just being together on weekends or seasonal breaks/vacations. But still, if one is relatively free of compulsive domestic work, one can still take pleasure in a child's company along with meeting work deadlines.

✦✦✦

I know it must sound strange to those living in the West, as everyone does their own chores there. In India, however, people are used to having domestic help.

Having said that, I must add that I have never been a stranger to domestic chores myself, having done a fair amount of it all my life, while growing up at home (since my mother refused to keep any help); after marriage, living with my in-laws; and especially in my decade in the Netherlands. But I have been out of touch for the last three years, after my return to Kolkata in 2017. Hence, my initial difficulty.

What has added to it is the lack of machines – there is no vacuum cleaner or dishwasher in the house, and even the rod of the long mop is broken! Thankfully, the washing machine is working. But on the other hand, the fridge is hardly used, as I am cooking fresh meals.

I am also cooking simple meals, but they have not been easy. Not at first, anyway. Exactly what I'm cooking and how much is extremely important, especially for my father. That's the secret of any good cooking, of course – a balance of flavours and ingredients. But for a kidney patient, not being able to do it right might be dangerous.

My first week of lockdown went in 'getting back' to cooking; more importantly, to cooking right. It is so easy to grow out of a habit; sometimes, I realized that in that week. Being inefficient, I spent practically the whole day in the kitchen, the first few days, and remained jittery throughout. By the end of the first week, however, my culinary skills were back in working order, and I got used to the rhythm of cooking and serving meals four times a day.

Every day in that week, I remembered that famous line from Tagore, summing up the general fate of women in his time (which has not changed for many even now): "Randhar pore khawa aar khawar pore randha" (Eating after cooking and cooking after eating). Remembered my mother doing it for all the 44 years of her married life, right until the day she died. Also, remembered myself doing it for several years in Amsterdam – the most difficult years being from S's birth to playschool.

So: cooking I got adjusted to during lockdown, but after a week, I still could not get all of it right together. When I managed the meals well, the cleaning (read sweeping/swabbing) suffered. The day I could do both, I could hardly give S any time. And of course, the most compromised was my own time (as it has been, unfailingly, for the last 8 years). Apart from what I gave to my students, i.e., Hence one night, I defiantly sat up, finishing a book I had started with great gusto before the quarantine, but had stopped reading in the intervening period; another sleepless night was spent in meeting a writing deadline.

✦✦✦

All these days, I have given myself Facebook breaks. I can see that the quarantined time is being spent by many to pause and reflect. People are full of helpful suggestions of how to spend the sudden gift of time: some are giving each other photo challenges (of one's sari-clad self, of oneself then and now, of travelled places, favourite books and films, fun questionnaires); others are either going back to, or stepping up, their passions – singing, dancing, drawing, exercising, photographing, sewing, you name it. All manner of interesting diaries are filling up social media space.

Some are evidently enjoying more time with family, or brushing up their culinary skills, or soaking up the quiet of otherwise noisy neighbourhoods; several have expressed the unexpected delight of hearing more birdsong. There are others who are recording with a sense of wonder the fresh flowers in their garden or clouds in the evening sky.

Some are more inclined to record the reality around them, their concerns and interests covering a wide spectrum: from reflections on the effect of the pandemic on students and their future prospects to what it can mean to writers, from feeding stray animals and helping those whose livelihoods have been affected, to sharing stories of doctors on the frontlines of fighting the pandemic 24/7, to the devastating news of thousands of migrant labourers walking for days and miles trying to reach home or others being sprayed with disinfectant to prevent contamination!

✦✦✦

I do not belong to either of these categories: I have neither given time to people/creatures in distress, nor given/accepted pleasant challenges to bide the time. Or seek respite from boredom. My problem is not a surfeit of time, but the lack of it. On normal working days, I race against the clock; during quarantine, I seem to be doing it even more.

I am just rushing from one work to another. Always a bit late, and always with a nagging sense of inadequacy; of not having done enough – not enough cooking, cleaning, teaching, giving time, looking after. In short, I am always falling short.

I am aware that there are many, even among those living in the shelter of their homes, whose situations are far worse than mine: people with babies, with bed-ridden parents, or sick family members having to go without medicine, the elderly left to fend for themselves, single men and women who live alone and are unable to travel to their families (like my own sister, braving it out in an apartment in Jersey City). This awareness is supposed to make me feel better about my comparative luck (it is a peculiar feature of the human mind that it needs to imagine worse in order to feel better). But it is not working with me. I still feel exhausted.

To have food on the table, a roof over one's head, a loved one nearby – these are luxuries in the present time. I know it. Still, I feel exhausted.

I feel small, petty, for feeling so. But the truth is, I am.

SHYAMBAZAR-ER MASHIMUNI (Aunt from Shyambazar) (17 April 2020)

"Tell me a story", S says in her sweetest voice, late one night. She says so every night. I mostly oblige. She is usually all ears and full of questions. Also, very often, after I am done, she ends up telling a story or two, herself: a mish-mash of cartoons she watches and her own vivid imagination. She expects to be complimented generously. I do. It is a sacred ritual. But it is particularly late this night and I am very tired. All I want to do is entwine her legs in mine, hold her close and go to sleep. But she simply does not allow that. "MAMMA, TELL ME A STORY", she hollers into my ears.

I start at that, but I cannot seem to remember any story from any book… anything at all. I tell her that, honestly… but she does not give up. "OK", she gets up, suddenly sitting upright in the dark, ready for negotiation, "tell me a story about your school". "I just told you so the other day", I remind her. "Tell me more", she demands. I am quiet. She changes her tactic now, trying persuasion this time: "Okay, tell me about your summer holidays". It strikes me that she is already treating the extended lockdown as a summer holiday… which it is, with all schools, colleges and universities in India now closed till June 10th.

Something happens to me then… my heart melts thinking of how well she has coped - given her tender years - with being at home for a whole month: keeping mostly to herself, studying fitfully, video-chatting with family and friends, trying to help me, sleeping more, and retreating more deeply into her imaginative world (read, drawing and talking to her 'pretend friends' much more). I give her a tight hug. My sleep has suddenly vanished… and I tell her about a favourite aunt of mine – Shyambazar-er mashimuni. She was an elder cousin of my mother, on the maternal side. And we usually visited her during our summer (and puja) holidays.

I tell S most of what I have recounted below…

✦✦✦

I don't know Mashimuni's name; ever since my childhood, it is the place where she stayed in Calcutta that has been her identifying mark for me. I can enter Sikdar Bagan Street (where she lived) blindfold… I had been there so many times. The whole family was an absolute favourite with us (my sister and me, that is) – Mashimuni, Mesho and Dadabhai, who was much older than us. In my childhood, I would borrow books from him – Alistair Maclean and stuff.

Mesho was one of six brothers, and they lived in a single room on the top third floor of a sprawling house situated in a narrow street, with a steep, narrow staircase. I could never understand why such a big house could not have more space on its stairs. I liked the spiral iron staircase that wound its way from the third floor to the big terrace upstairs, though, where Dadabhai would sometimes take us.

Since neither of the families had a telephone, we always went unannounced on afternoons - when the whole house was taking a nap - after watching a film at 'Minar' (Ma's indulgence after our annual exams). Though sometimes this rudely woke Mesho up a tad early from his siesta, he invariably greeted us with a wide grin and a big hug. Dear Mesho - with his twinkling eyes, white hair, and thin, wispy frame clad in neatly ironed-out white pajama and Punjabi - how we loved him! I often wondered how the family of three could manage to live in that one room. It was a big room, no doubt – with invisible partitions that designated different activities. At the centre was a huge Burma teak high bed. All the pillows and covers were stacked neatly at one end, against the headpost. At the far-right end of the room, in a long row, were a Godrej-almirah, an alnah for daily clothes, and a bookcase. And as you entered the room, on the left corner, was a small kitchen – basically for tea and the odd snack. The family kitchen was downstairs, on the ground floor, where everyone had common meals cooked by the two women of the house. Only two of the six brothers were married, so the house resonated with bachelor laughter and camaraderie – with cards and carom and adda.

One of them lived upstairs, in the room right next door to Mashimuni and Mesho – a big, healthy man, with a hearty laugh, with whom Mashimuni shared a special bond. Mashimuni bonded well with all the other younger male members of the family - her *deyars* - as well, and actually spent more time with them than with her husband.

Mesho was always pleased to meet us. He had already long retired from the gunshell factory that he had worked in by the time I was in kindergarten (the time of my earliest memory of that house), while Mashimuni, much younger than him, taught in a school. And since Mashimuni returned home only late in the afternoon, it fell to Mesho to make us tea, which he did lovingly. He would not trust that to anybody else. He made sweet milky tea, and then took out biscuits from an old Lactogen tin – so old, they must have been from Dadabhai's childhood. All the paraphernalia for making tea and snacks were arranged neatly in a small rack against the wall – tins, cups and saucers, bowls and glasses, the odd pot and pan. He in fact squatted on the floor to make the tea.

He was very fond of us and teased us no end whenever we visited. But he was fondest of Ma, having known her since she was a child. He was so protective about her that after her marriage, he would go to meet her at her in-laws every Sunday: he just wanted to make sure that she was doing well in her new family – the huge joint household that she had been married into. That, of course, stopped after a while, but Ma always remembered those early visits of his with the utmost gratefulness.

Whenever we visited, Ma and Mesho exchanged pleasantries, but it was only when Mashimuni returned home from work that the real conversations began. The two sisters always had a lot of catching up to do. Basically, enquiring about siblings and cousins and relatives, and people they knew. And at least one portion was devoted to recalling their Hazaribagh days, when Ma had stayed with them as a child. All kinds of embarrassing stories about Ma would surface then, so a bit of nostalgia always. Ma was 'bordi', the eldest sister, to everyone in her much bigger paternal family. But here, on the maternal side, she was the little sister, and indulged as such by her 'Didi-Jamaibabu', both so much older than her.

With every passing hour, the visit got more interesting. With Mashimuni coming, we usually had another round of tea, and then, with the coming of evening, Dadabhai brought what I most eagerly waited for: the evening snack! More often than not, it was either Chicken Roll or Mughlai Paratha – my favourite. I did not like egg much, but this avatar, I absolutely loved. Mesho took an evening bath unfailingly, and we went out on the terrace to chat – the three of us cousins.

Mashimuni and Ma had one thing in common – they both worried about widowed mothers and siblings who were not doing well. Both were just middle-class, but they were the best-off among their siblings, who were in much less fortunate circumstances than they, some with no stable incomes. The cousins actually came from vastly different backgrounds. Ma knew poverty from childhood, but Mashimuni was faced with reduced circumstances only much after her marriage.

She lost her father very young, but lived in plenty. A bachelor uncle ensured that – with a big house, servants, and an entire room for her. She was pampered and indulged by all. She married and first went to Allahabad; then, after a few years, came to Calcutta to live with her husband's family. There was no mother-in-law in the house, so the two sisters-in-law became mother figures. She was always a quiet person – elegant, soft spoken, and neatly dressed. Most of her education happened after marriage – her Intermediate, BA, and B.Ed., after which she joined a Primary School where she worked all her life. The working woman was not an entirely new phenomenon in Calcutta when she joined the school; hence, her work did not create a hue and cry, especially as the money was required. But her domestic duties and her role as *boudi* (elder sister-in-law) did not reduce one bit. She would stand for hours in the kitchen in the evenings, making rotis, after a full day of work and commute by public transport. In the mornings, she would cut the sabji and go. Ma had never heard her complain. She was - and remained till the last - exceptionally hard-working without anyone ever noticing it. She was never loud-mouthed or articulate about what she did; didn't have the kind of confidence that working women generally exude. Hers was a quiet personality.

✦✦✦

It is after ages that I thought about her... thanks to S!

"Do you have a picture of your Mashimuni?" she had asked me that night, after listening about her great-aunt.

I showed her a photo then – of didi and me with Mashimuni and Mesho – taken at a family wedding, most probably in 1996.

KAJOL (6 May 2020)

"Kemon achho go, didi" (How are you), she asks me, with a smile, broom and bucket in hand, as I hand over the previous day's garbage bag to her. I usually do not do this. My father does. Till four years back, my mother did – every day at 8 am, for all the 38 years that she lived in this flat in a small housing complex in North Kolkata. And for all those 38 years, at 8 am, Kajol came to pick up our bag and clean our building (Block B) after finishing with Block A and before going to Block C. She has continued with that routine almost four years after Ma's death (and that of several others in the complex); and I know she will do so till her death.

She is the cleaner, after all. She will have to work till the day she dies. Age brings no comfort to the likes of her. Life is what it always was, and will be.

When I was a four-year-old, trotting off to school at 6.45 am, I hardly saw her, because I would already be in school by the time she came to Block B. Sometimes, on weekends, I did catch a glimpse of her from our balcony – rushing from one building to another, her hair tied up in a severe bun sideways, her sari hitched up to her knees, her voice loud and raspy as she spoke to people always from afar (answering to some resident's question from a building she had just left or pissed off with the durwan's stupid joke). From afar, she always sounded angry and intimidating, but the moment she came into view, you would see a wide grin spread across her face, making you feel she is genuinely happy to see you. I have not seen that grin wane from age 4 to my mid-40s.

There are times I have wondered whether I am lucky with her smile because I have seen her so little in all these years: after school, things did not change much in my college-university years as well, at least as far as Kajol was concerned. I went to my institution much later than, no doubt, but also woke up late, much after Ma had deposited our garbage bag to her. And then for 18 years, I was away, first living with my in-laws in another part of the city, and then on a different continent. I did visit my parents during those years, but never stayed much with them. Kajol was never on my mind in those rushed visits or short stays.

It is different now, in the (almost) 3 years after my return. I see her every day, because she comes in just when I am rushing out with S, to drop her off at school and then on to work. She quickly gives me way if we happen to bump into each other, swiftly pushing her buckets away and widening her grin a tad bit more for S.

S loves to see her work on the day she does the building 'dhowa' – washing the wide landings on every floor with soapy water and then draining the water down, floor by floor. Though I want to save S from the dirty water pouring down the rails, the effect is actually not very different from rain on dusty streets or on our playground. The detergent used (no, it is not Nimyl or Lizol or any of the fancy disinfectants that we use at home) fills the air with a faint smell, and the landings look and feel wonderfully fresh when the water glistens on them, and clean after the water evaporates. S actually likes the exact same thing as I did as a child!

The last such 'dhowa' happened in mid-April – just before 'Poila Baisakh', the Bengali New Year. All our domestic help was on paid leave then, and continues to be so in the extended lockdown. Only Kajol cannot afford to have any.

We will not survive a single day without her.

CORONA + AMPHAN (26 May 2020)

Corona + Amphan is the worst double whammy one can think of; we are facing that at the moment. By 'we', I mean Bangladesh and two eastern states of India – Orissa and West Bengal. Cyclone Amphan hit us on 20th May. Last year, a similar cyclone - Fani - had hit the coastal belt lining the Bay of Bengal in early May. It coincided with my daughter's Birthday; hence, the small party I had arranged at home for her had to be cancelled. This year, a day after Amphan, with no internet, we could barely wish my niece in Hyderabad on her Birthday. While the ISD call did connect, all that could be heard from the other side were garbled voices... but at least, we could shout out a 'Happy Birthday'!

Privileged kids

Birthday celebrations are luxuries that can be done without for a year or two (though for children, it can be a bitter disappointment, eagerly wait as they do for months for their BIG day). But even for them, a greater calamity is not having access to TV or the internet. While 'connectivity' is an inevitable part of their lives even in normal times, it has been absolutely indispensable during the lockdown – both for work and play. Home-schooling has automatically increased the screen-time for most kids: in addition to TV programs and WhatsApp/Gallery photos and videos on their parents' mobiles, they have been attending regular online classes. A lot of the homework, too, is being necessarily done on the computer, as teachers send study material on Edmodo (often with a lot of YouTube and other links) and soft copies of worksheets to be worked on and submitted via email. While this exercise is increasing/improving the computer literacy of the kids, no doubt, they are left with very little work off-screen. Unless they practice things on their own… but that, obviously, is expecting too much from them!

In S's case, this has increased even more. With the printer at home not working, printouts cannot be taken – so she has ended up doing tasks on the machine that she would have otherwise written in long hand in her exercise copies. (That even those assignments would have had to be ultimately mediated through the parent - photos taken of the hand-written pages and then shared/forwarded in an email to the respective teacher - is a different story).

Unfortunately, though, just as she got more attuned to doing things online, Amphan hit us. It is the worst cyclone in the Bengal delta in more than 100 years. While it may belong to the same category of tropical cyclones as Fani, its impact on the ground has been far more severe. Its impact on families not directly affected by it, and on privileged children like S (yes, that qualification is very important), has also been very different. For Amphan has come as a profound irony: after two months of being wholly reliant on the internet, of being told "So what, you are at home? *everything* is still available at the click of a button", all of a sudden, kids have been thrown back to a pre-internet era existence, to an altogether different mode of being.

Throwback to a different era

As today's (22 May) edition of The Telegraph succinctly put it, Amphan has done what even Covid could not – snatch away even the solace of virtual connection from many people's lives.

The very fact that I quoted TT is because the newspaper is now my only link to the world. I read the paper after I do not know how long a time. Had almost forgotten how it felt like to hold it in my hands – opening out both arms to stretch the paper to its full length, and bending over a bit to read the text towards the top. Not just that; I also cut out a striking photograph from the front page of yesterday's edition (storm clouds gathering against the backdrop of the Hoogly bridge) and a feature I really liked in today's edition (where a well-known academic pleaded for a 'zero year' as a more practicable and fair solution to the academic crisis we are facing in India at the moment).

One naturally led to the other; or rather, was a natural corollary to the other – reading the hard-copy and cutting out the favourite bits, that is. In no time, I morphed back to my student self – when I would routinely cut pictures (rather randomly – of advertisements, writers, film stars, cricketers, heritage sites, you name it) and articles (op-eds from TT, and prior to that, innumerable features/interviews from 'The Miscellany', the beloved Sunday supplement of The Statesman).

This sudden, pre-internet era existence (admittedly, temporary), thus came in with a whiff of nostalgia for me, however irritated I might be at the inconvenience caused to my routine: cannot take classes or even record lectures, send emails, read online resources, catch up with news, call up loved ones, watch videos, not to speak of google-ing n-times a day for all manner of reasons.

The Betrayal

For my daughter (who just finished Grade II), however, and hundreds of thousands of kids like her (both older and younger), this sudden new mode of being is nothing short of a betrayal – for they are now being forced to realize that everything that has been promised to them can vanish altogether without warning.

Kids obviously have individual preferences: for S, the TV is more important than the internet, any day. Hence, it is not so much the virtual connectivity with others that she is missing these two days as much as bemoaning the fact that her chief source of entertainment - and frankly, of joyful sustenance - has been snatched away from her.

She did everything I reminded her that could still be done – read, draw, exercise, play (ludo), watch her favourite cats from our balcony. But even after all that, she asked me so many times: "Mamma, shall I see if the TV is working?" It is no use telling her it will not; she needs the testimony of her own fingers, repeatedly – the remote button pressed, but the slim black rectangular frame on the wall yielding forth no visual or sound.

It is difficult to convey the sense of desolation that TV-less days can bring to kids like S – who have no siblings at home or playmates where they live (the latter is out of the reckoning, anyway, during lockdown), and have working parents who can only give them 'quality time' ('working from home', unfortunately, does not change that much). Of course, in normal times, there are nannies – but they come and go, and can seldom, if ever, creatively engage with the child. Some also live with grandparents – once again, not all grandparents are the doting caregivers that they are stereotypically made out to be.

Peppa Pig, Dora, Masha and the Bear, Shimmer and Shine, Paw Patrol – they are just not programs with 20-minute slots, for S. They are her daily companions, allowing her entry into their fun-filled/adventurous/fantastic/magical lives (with a lot of outdoors, of course), and filling her imagination with stories which she recreates at bedtime or in English composition.

At school, she may study the explorations of Christopher Columbus and Vasco da Gama, create PowerPoint presentations on Rainforests, or try to figure out whether one-third is greater or smaller than five-sixth, or practice the difference between homonyms and homophones, not to mention learn poems by Tagore. It does not matter. Her academic progress has nothing to do with her entertainment. They just don't align. Her imaginary companions are simply her daily escape from a reality that is getting increasingly difficult to bear. Even for adults.

Counting one's blessings

9.30 pm. I have just started writing this piece. She comes and sits on my lap. I leave the typing and hold her tight. That always helps – both of us! With her head still buried in my left shoulder, she says: "Today also there was no phone, no TV… can I at least do my ballet class tomorrow?" I do not say anything about our snapped internet connection in reply. I just remind her of

Wednesday evening – with the storm raging outside and we sitting huddled together for a few hours without electricity. We faced that for only a few hours. There are many who are still facing it – having to manage without electricity, without water. We are much better off than they, I tell her. She has never experienced water scarcity in her eight-year-old life, so I am not sure whether she can fathom what it means. But the electricity part, she understands. The fan and the fridge are indispensable in summer – she knows *that.* And she could still do a PPT homework today on the laptop... she realizes that none of these would be possible without electricity.

Then I tell her of the lakhs (many times hundred thousand, I emphasize) whose homes have been washed away – their roofs blown off, all their belongings destroyed. Strangely enough, on the evening of the storm, panic-stricken, she had asked me precisely about them: "Mamma, what if our roof breaks?", she had asked first. I assured her it will not. There are two more roofs above us, all tight and secure, she need not worry. She then asked, "What will happen to the poor?" I must confess I did not expect that question from her. She has very little idea of the kind of poor people who lose everything in a storm. Our domestic helps are not poor – they are just people who belong to a low-income group, or else are facing reduced circumstances. But they all live in homes/rooms that cannot be blown away – though they may be shabby and small. Even the slum-dwellers that S passes by every day on her way to school have 'pucca' rooms now. S has watched the rage of the storm through glass windows on Wednesday, heard the howling wind despite everything being shut, seen our building being flooded that first night, photos of uprooted trees in the newspaper... but the devastation in our coastal areas... that is beyond the power of her imagination. Or, so I thought.

The very next morning, we heard of one such unfortunate home that was no more. A neighbour's driver told us about his aged parents in Namkhana, in the Sunderbans, being forced to take shelter in a local school, after their mud hut got wiped out by the cyclone. He was determined to take special permission from the police and travel to his village to stand by his parents.... but he could not get that permission.

S knows him well. I tell her his story as an example of what she had feared (on Wednesday) coming true. I tell her, again, that countless others are now without homes – like his parents. She goes to sleep with that thought.

I do not tell her the worst aspect of the double whammy of Corona + Amphan for these homeless people, though: in trying to seek shelter, they would face the palpable threat of Corona, as they would be overcrowded in whichever temporary shelter they hid.

I spare S the ultimate truth about human existence on this planet: no matter what the crisis (Corona or Amphan, or any number of calamities, natural or man-made, past or present), the poor are - have always been - dispensable.

RUNA (3 June 2020)

The electricity of the building was gone immediately after the storm hit Kolkata on 20th May. The balcony that serves as the entrance to their third-floor apartment in Salt Lake (bang opposite City Centre I) got flooded in no time, overflowing into the drawing room and her father's bedroom adjacent to it. It could not flow down to her bedroom and the kitchen at the back… but she had no time to feel thankful about it. Her father's room had to be cleared right away at any cost, for he would not sleep in any other; and she could not allow an 80-year-old man suffering from leukaemia to sleep in a room with rising water. She had to think fast. She first threw in as many heavy bedcovers as she could on the floors, to soak in as much water as was possible by the available fabric. She then got down to the task of clearing out the water with a long-handle mop – a difficult task as the wind blew hard and there was no light. She had two cell phones, but the torch of one was not working. She asked her 8-year-old daughter to hold the other phone-torch above her head, and told her father to stay the door with his hand so that the wind could not blow it shut as she kept pushing the water into the drain with all her might. This continued for a few hours; when she finished, it was past midnight. Her father got to sleep in his bed, after all.

For Runa, her father has always come first – before herself, her husband Sudhir, even her daughter Anaya. That is why she left what was in every sense a 'good life' - a successful career, a happy family, an active social life - in Riyadh, to come and look after her father in Kolkata. The year was 2016. What followed have been four very long years... and they seem to stretch away indefinitely…

This unusual choice was made by an educated, responsible daughter, out of an overwhelming sense of duty. Crucially, it was actually suggested by Sudhir, who continues to be supportive of Runa – though it has meant missing out on family life himself (except for holidays), missing out on seeing his daughter grow, and living alone in a foreign land.

Sudhir suggested what he did because it seemed to him the only solution at the time. In 2016, Runa's widowed father was diagnosed with leukaemia. He had been living alone since 2012, but it was not possible to leave him like that anymore. He needed an in-house care-giver, and Runa took it upon herself to be the one. Her younger sister, Ruchira, who had left for the US in 2007, was pursuing a Ph.D there. Runa was not willing to disrupt that, so she disrupted her own life. This was however not the first time that she prioritized her father. In 2010, when her mother died, she had come and lived with him for a year. Anaya was born in January 2012, and Runa got to live with her husband and child in Riyadh for the next four years – her 'bonus years', as she terms it. 2016 changed that scenario completely – she came to Kolkata and never returned.

The first casualty of that decision was her career – a flourishing banking career, spanning three cities and two countries. Runa had started working quite young in the late 90's after her graduation from Jyoti Nivas College (JNC) in Bangalore (her schooling had been in Kolkata, in La Martiniere) – first in Bank of America, then in ABN-AMRO in Pune (which is where she met Sudhir, then working for Citibank, at a bankers' meet), followed by a short stint in Standard Chartered in Kolkata, and finally HSBC

Insurance in Riyadh (after marrying Sudhir and moving with him to Saudi Arabia in 2006).

Sudhir is a Mangalorean Christian, Runa a Bengali Hindu. This could have been a potential problem, but was not. Starting a new life together in another country also went well for them – as both continued with their careers unabated and built a social life they enjoyed. Only, it could not last….

In one fell swoop, her father's disease changed everything for Runa. It changed everything for Anaya, too. She missed her dad, their home, their life in Riyadh. She did not like staying in Salt Lake, in an old house with an old man who could not engage with her. And she was furious that she could not live with her dad because her mom's dad was not well. Runa's father lives in the same building as his brothers, each with a separate flat. While Runa has a good equation with her cousins, the dilapidated building requiring heavy maintenance is a frequent headache for her. For Anaya, having no playmates her age in the building is a major deterrent. Runa's maternal home at Gurusaday Road - a spacious, cheerful place - is more amenable to both mother and daughter. No one stays in that house any more, Runa's grandparents having passed away and her uncle settled in the US. Runa and Anaya are used to spending the weekends there (Saturday morning to Sunday evening), but the lockdown has put an end to that, too. It has also squashed their summer holiday – the longest time that they spend together with Sudhir in the year.

The last four years has been incredibly tough for Runa: she is not only playing out the role of a dutiful daughter, but also, in effect, having to live the life of a single mom. Anaya's school routine - everything from pick up and drop to homework and extra-curricula's - is solely her responsibility, which in itself can be pretty exhausting. Her father's long servicing, live-in, male domestic help is helpful, no doubt, but his overall function, in terms of Runa's life, is restricted. There is just too much that only she can do; only she will have to do.

This year has been particularly cruel for her: her father's relapse earlier in the year has meant frequent hospital visits for chemotherapy. This came at a time when she was just thinking of taking up a job, at least something part-time (a resuming of the career she once had not being possible), especially since Anaya's school-time will increase from Grade III. But this modest plan, too, has to be shelved now. The chemotherapy is stalled at the moment due to the lockdown, but it will be resumed at the earliest possible opportunity.

As the walls close in on Runa from all sides – locked down in Salt Lake with no opportunity to escape to Riyadh on holidays, or seek weekly respite in Gurusaday in the city, or even think of a possible partial engagement during the day outside of home in the near future – there is one remarkable transformation that has happened in Corona times: Anaya has woken up to a new understanding of her mother's predicament and is eager to 'help' her these days. This is how children grow up – beyond height, weight, and body mass!

'PUPA' (27 June 2020)

Imagine this scenario: A son rushes to his home in Kolkata from the US to meet his dying mother, but misses her. After the period of mourning, he is about to head back when his father has a cerebral attack and goes into coma. He is hospitalized at first, but then brought home, as it is uncertain exactly how long it would take him (days/weeks?) to regain consciousness, if at all. What does the son do? You need to watch Indrasis Acharya's award-winning film *Pupa* to find out!

The son in the film is a young man, Subhro (Rahul Banerjee, probably in his career best), with a flourishing career in the US. His girlfriend, too, is all set to join him there (he is actually waiting for her to come and choose their apartment) with a job offer of her own. But going back to his life in the US would mean abandoning his comatose father to the care of unreliable nurses (working 12 hour shifts) and a 'boundule' bachelor uncle, his 'Kaku', Rajat Chatterjee (Kamaleswar Mukherjee in one of his finest performances), who is hardly ever present in their huge house – trekking with a group of friends one month, travelling abroad to attend a Conference on another, or else studying faces, cooped up in his room, if he does happen to be at home. There is the married elder sister, Mou (Sudipta Chakraborty, effortless as ever), of course, but she finds it hard enough to drop by at her father's every day, with a school-going kid, husband and mother-in-law to take care of in her other/own home; sustained care-giving, or rather, supervising the paid care-givers round-the-clock, is thus not possible for her.

Both Subhro and Mou test their limits for months, but cannot beyond a point. The sister is the first to capitulate: she had already earned the ire of her doctor husband for their daughter's lessened marks in class tests, owing to her negligence; but when he decides, with resolute conviction, that the child must not visit the depressing atmosphere of her natal home (although the child herself can barely stay without the mother and her presence livens up the sad household), she is left with no option but to stop her daily visits as well. Subhro, the bachelor brother, has no such socially acceptable escape route: he is racked between his genuine desire to fulfil his filial responsibility and the spectre of losing all that he has (his job, his girlfriend, a future in the US). He almost loses his mind in the process… until his uncle clears the way for him…!

Kaku is the emotional centre of the film, which explores Subhro's dilemma through the prism of this very special uncle-nephew bond – a bond that is fêted in our culture, always hovering somewhere between friendship and filial love. Feluda-Topshe, Kakababu-Shontu - the famed uncle-nephew duos of Bengali popular literature - always set off on adventures together, giving their avid readers high adrenaline, action-packed stories that became an integral part of their adolescence. In real life, however, the adventures are less mesmerizing; they are more journeys of the soul that a beloved uncle can help navigate, even in adult life. Like the one in *Pupa*. Kaku is the very embodiment of the cliché, "friend, philosopher, guide"; only, he is a philosopher with a difference – being both a stoic and an epicure. "If one is strong, one can live even with plants", he tells his nephew once, when the latter agonizes about his father's loneliness (just before his cerebral attack) – indicating that Subhro's mother's beloved house-plants could well be his father's companions in widowhood. "Do not mourn me when I die", he says another time, "just open a bottle of scotch and listen to Beethoven", which irritates his nephew no end.

Incidentally, all the trailer-worthy dialogues in the film are his, none more so than where he says: "Every relationship is a fine balance between investment and emotion". He wants his nephew to achieve that balance. The latter is however unable to, for unlike his uncle, he is built entirely in the traditional mould. Kaku's mentoring had clearly failed, Kaku regrets, in the face of Subhro's parents' sentimental middle-class conditioning. Subhro is furious hearing that, and has a massive showdown with his uncle, where the latter's pragmatism is pitted against his self-sacrifice. Kaku however terms that as "self-destruction", adding, "Self-destruction is brutality. If you lose this opportunity today, you will curse your father and he does not deserve that". His final argument is not an argument at all; it is a simple reckoning of the reality staring Shubro in the face, whether he wants to face it or not: "You have a bright future ahead of you. Life is calling you… and your father has already heard the call of infinity". It is clearly a choice between life and death.

At the end of the film, it may thus be safely assumed that Subhro could metamorphose into the new being that the film's title suggests. It is common to hear people say that a part of themselves died with a parent; *Pupa* demonstrates the other truth – that, it can be liberating, too. In fact, one can truly come into one's own only then.

Subhro's dilemma was resolved by his uncle; and though this film is about the conflict between personal desire and filial duty, we hardly get to see the filial relationship between Subhro and his father – even in flashbacks. That is because their relationship is not the point of the film; the moral duty such a relationship entails, is. The film dissects the social and personal ramifications of that duty.

✦✦✦

I watched *Pupa* on Addatimes the very day I heard its director speak in a webinar organized by our department. While watching, I could not help comparing it with Atanu Ghosh's *Mayurakshi* (2017), which has a somewhat similar storyline: a (middle-aged) son (who lives and works in Chicago) visiting his father in Kolkata, the visit prompted not by a death news, but a critical heath condition (the onset of dementia) in his octogenarian parent.

Soumitra Chatterjee and Prasenjit were both memorable as the father-son duo in the film, one slowly losing his mind to dementia, the other utterly lost in the peculiar complications of his life. Returning to his father is not even an option for Aryanil: he is twice divorced and has to maintain multiple households – his own in Chicago, his father's in Kolkata, his second wife's, in addition to the education of his son (from his first wife). He finds temporary solace while in Kolkata in the company of his best friend, Shahana (Indrani Halder, one of the delights of the film), but in general, is weighed down by life. His bond with his father is however special – it is both tender and affectionate, and not without humour. Most importantly, there is mutual understanding between them. He is extremely patient with his father's wandering mind; and the ageing/ailing man takes no time to gauge the sorrow of his son's lonely life. Dabbling with watercolours, he draws his son a window where he can sit when he is not feeling well! The son, in turn, while returning to Chicago, and leaving his father in the able hands of the efficient stay-at-home nurse (Sudipta Chakraborty), gives a false promise to the aged man – of taking him the next time – but breaks down in the airport. Nothing changes in their situation – apart from a renewed awareness that it cannot change.

Incidentally, in an interview with him, Acharya himself mentioned *Mayurakshi* as one of the best recent films he has seen. It may be noted that both the directors were, to some extent, drawing from their personal experience in these films: Acharya had returned to India in 2009 when his mother was diagnosed with cancer; Ghosh admitted in an interview that Sushovan, Aryanil's father in *Mayurakshi*, was inspired by his own. There are, in fact, two other recent films that also centre on the filial bond - Pratim D. Gupta's *Maccher Jhol* (2017) and Parambrata Chatterjee's *Shonar Pahar* (2018) - but they are mother-son reconciliation stories.

I am making these comparisons solely on the basis of theme and not styles of filmmaking (Gupta and Chatterjee's films are more mainstream, though both, in their own ways, are arresting in their storytelling). Each of them deserves separate analysis. I chose to focus on *Pupa* because it is the one that I saw last and because it has had the greatest impact on me. The point to note, however, is that a wide range of Bengali filmmakers have chosen to focus on the filial bond (albeit between a son and his parent) in the last few years. In three of them, the son lives abroad, comes home on an emergency and has to face a moral dilemma (either overt or subdued); more importantly, he is forced to measure his life in terms of his parent's (imminent/approaching/possible) death, and balance out the apportioning of guilt, love, and responsibility in his relationship with that parent.

I have known too many people living through various versions of this story in the last decade. It is, I will venture to add, one of the primary narratives of our time – this particular iteration of the filial bond, brought about by the forces of globalization. And it plays out particularly poignantly in a city like Kolkata, which can be said to be a huge 'Old Age Home'.

The pandemic has, however, changed (irrevocably?) both the practice and vocabulary of mourning, as it has the nature of relationships. Not being able to bid farewell to a parent when he/she breathes his/her last is now the new normal, as are rituals conducted over Zoom across cities/countries/continents. The conflict between desire and duty has been bulldozed over in a desperate bid for survival. Whether we metamorphose into a new being through this experience or not, only time can tell…

HAJAR-BUTI (12 July 2020)

Yesterday was not 'Mother's Day' or 'Women's Day', nor was it my Birthday or Ma's Birthday, or even her death anniversary – all the days on the calendar that I am supposed to specially remember her and miss her. And yet, Ma came visiting, in the most powerful way possible, as I chose to wear her saree for a workshop.

Wearing her saree was akin to wrapping a bit of her around me. I do consciously carry a bit of her on me on some (special) occasions – mostly jewellery, ear-rings, bangles, or chain (not that she had a lot!) - but yesterday, the choice had more to do with the weather (very hot) and the time I was supposed to speak in (afternoon, post-lunch). I wanted to wear something light (both in colour and weight) and formal. A much-worn *taat*, with an off-white base and a rich black-and-gold border, fitted the bill perfectly. I love this saree, love its simple elegance. But most of all, love the *hajar-buti* (a thousand dots) spread uniformly across the length and breadth of the nine-yard cloth!

I do remember Ma wearing this saree, but while choosing it, I did not give any thought to any other associations with it. They came tumbling forth only after I wore it...!

It must have been sometime in 2002... when Ma and I went saree shopping in Gariahat. A rare occasion. (The only two other such occasions that I recall were buying my wedding saree with Ma in 1999 and buying sarees for all three of us - Ma, didi and me - on a wedding anniversary of hers).

I was then a lecturer at Basantidevi College, a couple of tram stops from Gariahat Junction, on Rashbehari Avenue, and I lived in Kasba with my in-laws, with my husband away in Chennai. I went to my parents' every week – to unwind, recoup my energy, and indulge in my favourite food. Sometimes, I would watch the latest Bangla release with Ma, but never really socialized or shopped with her. So, this was special.

We went to 'RMGC Basak', opposite 'Pantaloons'. We chose it - or rather, Ma insisted on it - because it was reputed to be more 'reasonably priced'. I must say here that, by then, I already had my own favourite saree shops in Gariahat: 'Trader's Assembly' for wedding gifts, 'Kanishka's' for tasser, 'Jamdani Ghar' for (you guessed it right) jamdani, 'Jaylakshmi' for pashminas/silks and chiffons, 'Asha Brothers' for south cottons, AND, most importantly, pavement hawkers for *taat* and printed sarees that could be bargained for. My sister-in-law was a huge fan of these pavement collections, but my mother's love of them was of a different order. Of all the sarees I gifted her, her most prized possession was a *taat* bought from a hawker who sat right at the entrance of my college. Reason: it was priced at Rs.130/! It would have been priced at least double, if not treble, in any shop, Ma would never tire of saying. That was probably true; and it is not that Ma habitually bought sarees from pavements (most of her collection was from a few trusted emporiums in 'Uttarapan'), but it was because of the low price of that saree that she loved it so much! She was always trying to save money – first Baba's, then ours (she had very little of her own after she left her full-time lecturer's job to bring us up): that irritated me no end.

So, we went to Basak, with me making Ma promise beforehand that she would ignore the price tag while choosing her saree. For once, she did; mostly because the prices were so low, anyway! We both bought a few, this *hajar-buti* being one of them. Ma had at least a dozen sarees of this combination – but in different weaves and styles, thanks to the immense variety of cottons from different states of India. This was a *taat*, priced somewhere between Rs. 350/ and Rs. 420/. It was above the range Ma allowed herself to buy cottons, but she relented this one time, after I persuaded her that she, too, could gift me a similar one. This exchange offer worked: I gifted her this saree, and she gifted me another *hajar buti*, which had white 'butis' on a mauve base and a deep purple-and-gold *paar*/border. It still has pride of place among my *taats*... so precious that I have hardly worn it. We bought quite a few sarees that day, unusually so, but I remember only one other among them – a peach 'dure' (priced at Rs. 230/) which I wore to college often.

Saree was my uniform in college. Back then, that was the norm. It was the only formal that was accepted. Forget western wear, even the wearing of *salwar-kameez* had to be fought for, or at least, explained. That was the case at least in West Bengal. And it was also the most common gift that adult/married daughters received from their mothers. I got a new saree from Ma every year – on my Birthday, Anniversary, *Jamai-shasti*, *Nabo-borsho* and *Pujo*! They are all wasted now in Godrej *almirahs* I am finding increasingly difficult to maintain. The silks and chiffons of my collection were amply used in my decade in the Netherlands, for every social and academic occasion I could find an excuse for wearing. But strangely enough, I have no time for them after my return to Kolkata: early working hours, added responsibilities in the mornings, and a general growing out of the regular habit of wearing sarees have all contributed to it. I need a lot of motivation to dress up in a saree these days, with the result that events/formal occasions apart, I usually do not. When I do, however, they usually turn out to be either Ma's sarees or ones gifted by her!

She remains with me. *Hajar smriti jure....*

GOROM BHAAT (29 July 2020)

I must confess that when it comes to food, there is nothing more visually appealing to me than a plate of steaming white rice – preferably on a white plate. Also, to please me, it must be what in Bangla we say 'jhorjhore bhaat' – which means, the rice should be steamy but not sticky, with every grain separate from the other, moist and yet dry.

Boiling the rice to the right extent and draining it out at the right time are key factors here. Refined rice is another requirement – the colour will not be white otherwise; and instead of long, slender white grains, one will have brownish-yellow, fat, round ones. Cooking this perfect rice, like cooking any other food, can be achieved only with practice. I had achieved that when, for 10 years in Amsterdam, I cooked it almost every day – the rice extra white and fragrant, because it was Basmati.

I would mostly cook rice in the evening, when the sun set in a riot of colours. Late afternoon was usually a blaze of yellow, but in the early evening, pink, violet and fuchsia took over. I could never describe that colour, that particular combination; could never articulate to anyone what that did to me. I also never tired of the sight. Of its sheer beauty: elusive, ephemeral, indescribable. In that magic hour, the light would fall in huge, wide swathes over the entire apartment; its spacious, neatly rectangular rooms, each a different colour – tender green, bright pink, clear blue, light brown. But the kitchen was white: white walls and doors matched by white cupboards on both sides and white tiles near the oven. Only the double-door fridge was grey. Its shiny surface caught the light and dispersed it at an oblique angle in the kitchen. In time, that play of light became an integral part of the cooking of rice for me.

✦✦✦

Rice is our staple food. The history of the region I come from is rife with the history of hunger, its colonial history especially defined by successive famines, the most heinous of which was the Famine of 1943. Growing up, the images of cultural memory that made the strongest impression on my mind were artwork, film stills and fiction passages that document/represent/memorialize/historicize that hunger. Result: when I think of rice as part of our cultural history, I invariably think of the lack of it.

I have never known that lack. My mother had… and would tell my sister and me stories of how her family's meals would often be not rice, but rice gruel, with nothing to go with it but salt. That was, very often, all her young widowed mother could give her seven hungry children, ranging between toddler and teen, when suddenly one night her husband died at the hands of dacoits, leaving them destitute. Later in life, as a working woman, and then a wife and stay-at-home mother of two, Ma would cook refined rice every day of her life – just the right texture. With all the maddening variety of tasty Bengali food that could go with it. She loved cooking and feeding others – took a natural delight in it that I have not inherited (though didi has). I remember Ma slogging in the kitchen, pouring her creativity into the daily act of feeding and sustaining her family, just as she made an art of every other domestic chore. But I do not have any specific memory of her cooking rice; just how it looked on our plates when it was served.

My memory of my own cooking, however, somehow congeals around the cooking of rice. There are countless images saved in my drive related to our kitchen/food/meals/hospitality, but this is what I remember the most: evening, pink rays filling up the kitchen, creating undulating geometric patterns on the fridge door facing the light. And I am cooking white fragrant rice.

✦✦✦

An Iranian couple with two children bought our apartment, I was told. I never met them, but I have often thought of them in the last three years. Does the wife stand at the same spot that I did, cooking rice for her family at the same time in the evening? Does she, too, get distracted by the beauty of the hour? Probably… I don't know. What I do know, however, is that 'property' can be bought and sold, but the memory of 'home' stays forever. And though the 'ownership' (or rather 'proprietorship') of home has to do with money, the sense of 'belonging' to it can only come with love for a particular space and one's lived experience in it.

TILL DEATH DO US PART (3 August 2020)

"Sometimes, I worry... if she dies first, what will happen to me?"

This fear is voiced not by a spouse or partner, but by a sister – in Tanuja Chandra's latest film, *Aunty Sudha Aunty Radha*, a documentary on her two elderly paternal aunts who live together in a village close to Delhi. The film is part of this year's online NYIFF and is available on MovieSaints for a few days. I had difficulty logging in, which was a great disappointment this weekend. But even the three-minute trailer left a mark on me ... and compelled me to write this piece.

I was moved because it resonated with me. This is, after all, what I ask myself frequently… have asked myself most in the past few months. If anything were to happen to didi (my sister), how would I live?? For as certainly as I know that the earth is round, and that night is followed by day and winter by spring, I know that I cannot do without her. Does not matter that oceans lie between us, that even an annual meeting is too much to ask for, that we will always miss out on each other's special days, that I will bring up a child without ever having the comforting presence of either my mother or sister near me, that we will actually never live together. Does not matter. Because I know, when I need her, she will be there. Always. From convincing Baba to agree to my marriage when I was quite young to standing in for Ma when S was born 13 years later, from gifting me a holiday when I was almost losing my mind in my mid-30s to standing by me when I started afresh in my early-40s, to financially supporting my dream project… she has been there for everything that really mattered to me.

21 years we have lived apart: first in different cities in India, then in different continents - in two glittering capitals of the world, New York and Amsterdam - leaving Ma forlorn in Kolkata. At one point, we fantasized living together in our old age… maybe in adjacent flats, for we fight too much for us to survive in the same space!! After Ma's death in 2016, that fantasy should have given me renewed hope… but, ironically, that is precisely the time I realized that we are destined to live apart. I have made my peace with that reality now.

But I have seen other sisters, across three generations - my grandma's, Ma's and mine - who have been both mentally and physically close, living in the same city/town/neighbourhood/building, sharing lives in ways that are never possible long-distance. This is true of all relations, not just siblings. But there is something about the intimacy of the bond between sisters that renders it particularly desirable. I have heard numberless women of varying age vouch that their sisters are the closest person in their lives, and that they would like to live together, or at least close by, in old age – if they do not do so already. I have seen the truth of this statement borne out in the lives of women dear to me: my *dida* (maternal grandmother), who lived walking distance from two of her sisters in Habra; same for my *mami* (maternal uncle's wife); my sister by marriage, who lives one floor below her sister in Hyderabad; my dearest aunt (outside family relations) whose sister lived one floor above hers in Kolkata (till last November). This is not to say that I have never seen soul-mate brothers, or soul-mate brother-and-sister; I have, but soul-mate sisters seem to outnumber them easily.

The sisters I am referring to are, however, not just one's own siblings, but also cousins or friends who have been an integral part of one's life for a long time. In fact, given the number of people growing up in nuclear families since our generation, friends are increasingly the only family one is left with. Both didi and I have another sister we cannot do without – our respective besties. Here, too, the fantasy of living close by in old age is strong. In my case, once again, I have accepted the impossibility of it; but didi might still end up with her bestie somewhere in the US. (Save for me, all three of them live there).

This brings me to the question: what about those who do not have siblings or friends they want to die with? And what of them who cannot rely on their partners to hold their hands in old age? I am afraid the latter category is the invisible majority. For, far before death parts partners, life does. Some parts amicably, some bickering all the way. Still others live separate lives in the same house. The only lucky ones are those who genuinely live together – though it is a luck that is always hard-earned.

We are conditioned to believe in 'happily ever after'; the 'death do us part' is a natural corollary to it. We aspire to that condition, and are invariably left distraught when it turns out differently for us. We give far more importance to romantic love and marriage than they deserve – because, in the final analysis, neither romantic nor marital relationships are life-sustaining, for a vast majority of people. The ones that are - the loyalty/solidarity of friends and siblings - are not eulogized obsessively in poetry and song and film. That is because we tend to take these relationships for granted… until we are left alone.

Maybe it is time that we gave these other kinds of love in our lives their due.

'GOING' TO SCHOOL... (24 August 2020)

Five whole months at home! When the first lockdown was announced for three weeks on March 22nd, it seemed very long. And now, we have stayed indoors for more than twenty. The only time we went out was when S was suddenly down with fever in early July and had to be taken to the doctor. Thankfully, it was nothing serious. She recovered in a few days... and touch wood, has been fine since then.

But it is getting increasingly difficult to keep her at home. And I am feeling increasingly fatigued even on weekends. I long to press the pause button in my life; she desperately waits to go back to school. Neither is possible.

It goes without saying, I'm worried about her waiting any longer. Especially since she has taken it into her head that her school will reopen in September. I know it will not. It cannot. The school has definitely not given any such intimation. Still, I quickly checked with a friend – one of her classmates' moms - and of course the answer was 'No'. I felt relieved and sad at the same time!

Her new session at school began full-fledged from 6th July: 6 classes every week day (7, if you take the 15-minute class teacher's time at the beginning), from 8.45 am to 1.30 pm, with two breaks. Two weeks later, the new semester started in my college as well, so that our home looks more like a coaching centre now – with her learning in the drawing room and me taking classes in the bedroom (a thing I don't like at all). I also had to buy a new laptop because the old, spare one had stopped working; and given our simultaneous classes, and her online assignments in addition to all my work, we just could not afford to share one laptop anymore.

She started Grade III on a great note. "Uff, FINALLY, FINALLY, Mamma…", she told me once, unable to continue in her sheer excitement. "'Finally,' what, beta"? I asked. "FINALLY, my life has BEGUN"!! Reason? She could - finally - use the laptop herself! She felt a tremendous sense of purpose and importance when, a few days into her new session, I allowed her to open her laptop – to type in the password, i.e., hitherto not known to her. That gave her a delicious sense of freedom! Even more adventurous was to enter the LMS platform (the online system her school is following) on her own, from her new school Gmail account. The uploading/downloading of material was another matter: that took some practice!

The six weeks of school till now has gone well. I can hear her morning classes from our adjacent kitchen and dining room, and can clearly make out that she enjoys her lessons. She is very happy, though, to let go a few minutes early, or on the rare occasions when a teacher cannot take a class: she comes to me for a quick hug then, or runs to the balcony to talk to her 'pretend friends' (a secret sisterhood I am not supposed to know anything about). She likes all her subjects, but at the moment, is especially drawn to Spanish, her new subject this year. I think it is primarily because of her long love of 'Dora, the Explorer' and hence her sonic familiarity with the language that Dora uses. (She corrected my pronunciation of 'parapata' while we watched *Dora and the Lost City of Gold* two weekends back). Overall, I see her enjoying her studies in Grade III far more than I have in the last three years

– sitting down to do her homework soon after lunch sometimes, or looking up something online on her own (a video of a singing skeleton holding forth on the 206 bones of the human body was a recent favourite)!

The classes are fine: the first half of the day just flies away with her wonderfully preoccupied. I feel very grateful for that. Initially, she was very happy to meet her friends and teachers online. That seemed natural enough, after the six weeks of her summer vacation spent entirely at home this time. Anything was better than that. But I have sensed a restlessness in her the last few days… punctuated with plans of what she will do "when I go to school in September": which frocks she will wear, what tiffin she will take, the new stationery she needs, the cards she will gift her friends. All of which ends with the phrase, "Okay, Mamma"? I of course say "Okay", and play-act an excitement that I know will be difficult to keep up with in the coming months….

A TEACHER'S 30 YEARS' BATTLE AGAINST CORRUPTION (5 September 2020)

In 1960, a young Physics lecturer joined Surendranath (Day) College in Calcutta. Not long after, he discovered, to his great shock, that the Governing Body (including eminent educationists, scientists and legal luminaries) managing the affairs of the Surendranath group of institutions was involved in financial malpractices: it siphoned huge amounts of money away from the College fund to the fund of the Trust, thereby considerably retarding the development of modern scientific education in the College.

It dawned on the lecturer that this state of affairs had continued unabated for several years because the Managing Committee was being protected by some provisions made in the Calcutta University Act of 1966, and he realized that unless these provisions were changed, the condition of the institution would not improve. What was called for, in fact, was a fundamental change in the basic nature of the management – from being an effectively autocratic body to a fully democratic one. At stake was the very future of the College: the academic interests of its students and the welfare of its employees, including both teaching and non-teaching staff.

Something had to be done and this idealistic young lecturer took the lead. It all started as a single man's protest against the rank corruption of the GB of an undergraduate College, but gradually gained momentum and grew into a full-fledged 'andolan' (movement); involving a protracted legal battle that began in the late 1970s and continued till the late 1990s, after which the Governing Body of Surendranath College was eventually, formally democratized. The benefit of this movement was also shared by 41 other Colleges in West Bengal that were run by a Private Trust.

✦✦✦

This is a very insignificant tale in the grand narrative of India's postcolonial history and will soon pass into oblivion. Probably, it already has.... save for two slim documents, copies of which are in the safe custody of the lecturer's younger daughter: one is the WBCUTA (West Bengal College and University Teachers' Association) News Bulletin of July 1998; and the other, the 1996 issue of Surendranath College Magazine.

The former gives a vivid description of the protracted legal battle of the Surendranath College Trust vs. the University of Calcutta, highlighting WBCUTA's consistent support to the latter; while the College Magazine pays tribute, in its editorial, to that fearless Physics lecturer who had recently retired: Prof. Birendra Narayan Roy - 'Biren' to his friends, 'BNR' to his students. Calling him "the pioneer of Surendranath College's anti-Trust andolan", the editor goes on to say that the College "will be forever indebted to this most single-minded and humble of men, for engineering its overall development since 1977"; and that he "won't be guilty of exaggeration if I term 1977-1997 as 'Birendra jug' (the Birendra period) in the history of Surendranath College".

BNR himself dismisses this tribute as hyperbole, saying that the long struggle and ultimate victory could not have been possible without the support of friends, colleagues, and powerful well-wishers; but he does admit that those two lines are THE ONLY formal recognition of his three-decade-long struggle against the Trust.

Indeed, 'College' and 'Court' had become inextricable entities in his life. He gave his prime and all his money (which was not a lot, anyway) to the cause. Neither had mattered much to him. But on the altar of his idealism was sacrificed another invaluable asset – his wife's aspirations. Herself a lecturer (in Bengali), she gave up a most promising career, pawned her jewellery for him and devoted herself to their two children so that he had the time and the means to do what he felt compelled to – unhampered.

✦✦✦

On Teachers' Day (celebrated in India to commemorate a great teacher and philosopher, Dr. Sarvepalli Radhakrishnan, India's first President), I pay homage to those thousands of anonymous teachers (past and present) who had/have selflessly devoted themselves to an institution, putting its welfare and improvement before their own careers. And I salute all those friends/associates/partners who have silently and steadfastly supported them.

✦✦✦

PS: This is actually a re-post from 2014.

The story remains exactly where it was six years back.

The younger daughter, at the time she first wrote this post, was trying to retrieve this story from oblivion and record her father's testimony... but it never proceeded beyond a few phone calls – living as she did on another continent. And even that exercise was a tall task and resembled more like the young Hindi lecturer in Anita Desai's *In Custody*, trying to record the Urdu poet Nur's voice and life story. It was an exercise in futility, destined to fail... as too much stood in the way. In this case, it still does. The daughter now lives with the father, but is too enmeshed in - and tired of - her own struggles to give time to his lost story.

As for the father, now widowed, he potters around the house, looking a strange cross between Einstein (fizzled hair) and Santa (long white beard), obsessed with his daily routine of eating/sleeping/having medicines. Most of his friends and associates have died, and the College that was everything to him once is now a blur....

400 WORDS A DAY (11 September 2020)

"A 400-word day is a beautiful day" – thus spake Tanuj Solanki! This was sometime last year, and he wrote it in response to a Facebook post by Michelle D'Costa, on writerly anxieties. After all these months, and hundreds of posts later (read/browsed through/scrolled down), I still remember this one. Partly because I have read very few honest posts on Facebook about the vulnerabilities of the writing life – frequent rejections, endless waiting, a gnawing sense of inadequacy, the indifference of the world, iniquitous recognition (if at all), among others. Michelle was laying herself bare in this post in a way few do – in this instance, about her inability to write as much as she targeted. But what made it even more memorable for me was the response by Tanuj. It was a long text… but that phrase jumped out at me. It was meant to console, reassure. I was, however, most moved by the tone: both tender and affectionate, it was a voice that was a cross between a mentor and a friend. Only the writer-friend of a writer can do this, I thought!

T.S. Eliot had said that the best critic of poetry could only be a poet. That any art could best be understood by a practitioner. He was talking primarily of the reception of art, but I think something of the same logic can be applied to the production of art as well. Nothing like the solidarity of fellow artists while one is hammering away, at whatever…! I can vouch for this myself. I felt this most keenly with my writing-group friends in Amsterdam. *Gariahat Junction* would not have happened otherwise. In Kolkata, I continue to write, of course, though I am not a part of any writing group here. Truth is: I would not have been able to attend a single session, had I been. So, I have no regrets! I do have writer-friends widely dispersed across the globe, though, with whom I am well connected through Facebook. Gives me a sense of community to read and respond to their posts, and get their feedback on mine.

The significance of this community has only increased during the pandemic, when the entire eco-system around writing has undergone a drastic change, like with all the other arts; in fact, all other fields of human activity.

It was a great coincidence, therefore, when, a couple of months back, I read a repeat advice in an article by Vikram Chandra. Talking of his own practice, he said he aimed at 400 words every morning, after editing the previous day's work.

I have agonized about the utter lack of time to write during these lockdown months… then, in a private aha-moment, I told myself I will follow the 400-word rule, and let Tanuj know he has done me a huge favour (without knowing it) by setting a do-able target. I have been trying this… with occasional success. But just when I thought of sending him a text, I saw a 'Story' by him: "Stoic selfie-face after worrying the whole morning if I will ever be able to write again and writing precisely 16 words".

I was supposed to feel bad reading this, but it had a very different effect on me… I felt less alone in my misery. Told him so. As I wished him more productive days ahead, he responded with disarming good humour: "The target for tomorrow is 17 or more"!

This morning, I managed 560 words. Though I basically wrote about not being able to write, I am absolutely sure I am going to have a great day!

PRIVILEGED/ENABLED DOMESTICS
(17 October 2020)

A full seven months into the pandemic, I have realized a new reality in India. While migrant workers have been the hardest hit, some of their cohorts in the city have done well. This realization came in the wake of the powerful image that went viral yesterday – of Ma Durga as a migrant worker with children in tow, by the artist Pallab Bhowmick.

By 'cohorts', I am referring here to the daily migrants who commute to the city from the suburbs by train. When the first lockdown was announced in India in late March this year, they were distraught because it meant they would lose their daily wages. With successive lockdowns in the next few months and train services closed, their livelihoods were threatened. However, there were at least some who managed not only to survive but also did not face any trouble at all, as they were given paid leave by their employers. Which is how it should be. I know because we are one of the employers who did so, as have many others of my acquaintance who hire domestic staff - help, cook, nanny, nurse - from ayah centres; workers who are paid by the hour, and whose rates are way higher than local helps, as a certain percentage of what they earn has to be given to their centre.

Domestic circus since 2017

These 'centres' have been my lifeline since autumn 2017, when I started living with my widowed father after returning from Amsterdam. He was already living alone for a year then. And my mother's absence had been replaced by a bunch of domestics

– day help, cook, someone who did the grocery, and a part-time driver. After I returned home with a child, a nanny was added and a full-time driver was engaged. And after my father suddenly fell ill with a kidney problem just a few months later, nurses had to be included to this ever-increasing group: two at the beginning for a few months, for 12 hours each, when Baba was bed-ridden at home after six weeks in hospital; and then one, when he slowly got back on his feet again. At some point, the previous domestic help, Soma, doubled up as the night nurse.

To coordinate this staff daily has itself been a full-time job. There is not a single week when someone or the other is not absent or does not have a problem. They are all people with families, after all, and most of them are women with children; they are often left at the mercy of vagaries at home. And I, in turn, am left at their mercy. I have often felt that my teaching is actually a secondary activity: my real 'job' is to keep this staff going.

In the first year after my return, I lost count of how many people joined and left: there were three of S's nannies who followed each other in rapid succession, and Baba's day/night nurses changed up to four times (if I remember right). I also lost count of just how many times a day the door had to be opened… because there was not a single hour when the calling bell did not ring. Between them, from morning 7.00 to evening 8.30, our house staff constituted a long chain of arrivals and exits (7.00 am -12.00 noon being the peak time) – one coming as the other prepared to leave, some overlapping; and interestingly, managing to have even in those small pockets of time some very spicy relationships, rife with jealousies and rivalries, tiffs and showdowns. TV soaps paled before them!

When Baba was alone, nobody (in the then smaller staff) was ever absent. They had great concern for this 80-year-old man living all by himself, who was still agile and active, and who really did not need much looking after. Their workload was also less, as there was little to do in the house. But things changed after I came to stay, with a child. Their absences increased, for one, especially the cook's; and the dynamic at home also changed. Drastically so, when Baba was taken ill. All through this, Soma remained the most reliable worker at home and continued to be so till March 2020.

White collar slavery

During the lockdowns, none of our house staff could come. While we gave paid leave to all, our need for all of them was not the same: while the driver was not required at all (since we were not going anywhere) and the nanny could also be done without (as I was at home), the cook and the day help-cum-night nurse were very important for us. After two months of paid leave, we asked the latter - Soma (name changed) - to stay with us. That way, she could easily maintain her job and I would be spared the tremendous extra workload that had befallen me. She was used to spending more than half the day with us, anyway. We suggested that for the next few months (things were still very uncertain), she just extend that and make it full-time work. She accepted it rather reluctantly. Her father died suddenly, soon after, so she left again to be with her bereaved family. We thought she would return after the 'sraddho' ceremony, but she did not. She had left for good.

She was with us for only a fortnight – all the while restless, unhappy. She was free for half the day, could call her sons anytime, see them every day on video, but I could sense her restlessness… though I had never expected that she would leave without notice. Her father's sudden loss, we respected: giving her 14 days off soon after she joined. And then waiting for her return. The whole of June went by in waiting and hoping for her return. I have waited for a few people in my life the way I waited for her in June – both for Baba's sake and mine.

Who leaves a secure job at a time when so many others are losing their incomes? It can only happen if an alternative source has been arranged. She said she cannot live without her sons. But none of them do any work: they were both looking for one, the last I knew; one after graduating, the other after not having finished his degree. The three of them living happily together for months with no food on the table made no sense. Plan B was obviously in place.

I find people in white collar jobs faring far worse. I know of experienced journalists who have been unceremoniously sacked, part-time teachers who have not been paid for months, IT professionals who have had massive salary cuts. In my family, salaries have either been slashed, or late in coming, or both. I also know that nobody among my friends/acquaintances is even dreaming of greener pastures, because there aren't any. People are simply holding on to their jobs, even the ones that pay abysmally, because losing them would be worse.

Among our house staff, the most reliable one left (who worked for two); the cook (who in any case is frequently absent) is only waiting to go back to her family in Bangladesh (which she has been doing since she lost her brother last year); the nanny (the most well off among them) has 'decided' she will not work during the pandemic (as she is saddled with everything at home - kid, in-laws, house-work); and the driver (the most needy of them all) has come religiously right at the beginning of every month to claim his salary with what can only be termed 'swag'! I am the only one among them who both needs my salary and has to work to earn it every month.

Glad…

I gave Soma two relaxed months. I am glad that they were the only ones in her life. When mornings were spent having tea at different neighbours'; housework and lunch completed, post lunch was time for ludo, picnic style - lying on newspapers, under the shade of a tree, munching on savoury delights; and evenings were devoted to cooking her sons' favourite dishes (this part she loved, as they could never have dinners together while she worked). When she recounted her blissful lockdown weeks to me with evident relish, I would recall the frantic/feverish ones I had had – paying her and doing her work, and those of others. In addition to mine, of course.

My friends, family members and I have had to work more during the pandemic – no matter which profession we are in. We worked more, got the same or less or late salary, or were sacked. And here she was, talking about lazy afternoons full of ludo and cucumber salads and tamarind chutneys. I did not say anything to her about the disparity of our situations in those months… was just *relieved* that she was now with us. Mostly, for Baba's sake.

Feeling betrayed

Baba is always kind to a fault and generous with financial assistance to needy people. And I have not known a more compassionate man than him when it comes to domestic help. His care and concern for them far outstrips what they do for him or the house. This is especially so with the ones who came into his life after Ma's death: he would insist on buying Women's Horlicks for them, and tears would well up in his eyes, speaking of the injustices they had faced in life. He was extremely fond of S, looked on her like a daughter (she also happens to be exactly my age). He also relied on her a lot; no one was happier than him when we decided to bring her home to stay with us. Having worked for him since 2016, she knew his routine inside out: what he ate, what he wore, his medicines, his idiosyncrasies. He would chat with her while she worked; she would scold him for being unreasonable sometimes. We looked upon her as a family member, and were both partial towards her, because she was sincere in her work and also chipped in when others were absent.

I have always looked upon the women who have worked for me as co-workers, because their work in my home has enabled mine outside it. Over the last three years, Soma was the one who had been witness to my daily challenges, and helped me navigate them; I gradually came to look upon her not only as a co-worker, but a friend. One of my earliest posts in my blog was about her:

that is the respect I accorded her and her life. At the end of each day, we would sit and chat – two working mothers, with different-aged children. I genuinely thought she would continue working for us: she was good at her job and earned a substantial income. I thought it worked well both ways; that the comfort level was on both sides. I was wrong. Turned out… we were just another employer for her!

The positive side

I tried to see the positive side of things after she left. To begin with, because of her, I could go out of the house three precious times during the initial lockdown months, which I would not have otherwise. Never mind that they were taken to the police (local Police Station and then to the Head of Traffic, Lalbazar), to the doctor (more than once actually), and to bring her. The first two were for permissions, the third to ensure that she had a safe passage from her home to ours. The day I chaperoned her, I had felt a real sense of achievement! I had fallen ill in May… out of sheer exhaustion, but this had to be done. And a whole excited week went by arranging to bring her back.

After she left, from July on, with S's new session in school and my new teaching semester at college in full swing, my work increased manifold. But I did not fall ill from exhaustion anymore… because I realized that is not an option available to me.

The other truly positive thing that emerged out of this situation was that both S and I became more self-sufficient: I simply morphed back to an earlier self who was used to doing compulsive domestic work, while S learnt to bathe and eat lunch herself!

Enabled few

Four months down the line, I see this issue even more differently. To return to where I began: the powerful image of Ma Durga as a migrant worker.... it is good to see that at least some workers have options and can exercise their right of choice. They are paid according to their experience, with a mandatory increment every year: as per their experience, expertise and working hours. They get paid leave, and they leave good employers to work for better ones. Most importantly, they have the confidence to do this during a pandemic. Because they know their services are required.

I am happy that at least some women are having it good, after years of struggle. May their tribe increase!

SNACKS FOR MEALS (29 October 2020)

"I keep writing shorter stuff to allay the hunger of my writer soul… but snacks can never stand in for full meals!"

I wrote this to Saikat Majumdar in one of our earliest, and longest, conversations to date. The original context of it was Saikat's highly sensuous novel *The Scent of God,* and my initial response to it in an email to him… from where we drifted to the writing life in general. Only, I did not seem to have one: my maiden collection of shorts had been accepted for publication for more than a year then, but I still did not know when it would come out; and a work-in-progress epistolary novel on which I had worked for two years had been shelved for the next two. Trying to find a toehold in Kolkata professionally after a decade abroad, and settling my daughter down in a new environment had taken more time than I had imagined; whatever was left of my energy was invested wholeheartedly in a dream initiative – the Kolkata Partition Museum Project. Hence, my writing suffered. Since I was unable to work on the novel, I settled for a blog: snack for a meal!

I have survived on that snack – KOLKATA DIARIES – for two years now! I started it in early February 2018, with 'Back to Presidency', which dealt with what I felt about coming back to Presidency as a teacher, 25 years after I left the institution as a student. I was still relatively new in my comeback then. Just six months. Soon after, even my new reality would change irrevocably, as the person I most banked on in Kolkata - my father - would be hospitalized, and then bed-ridden for months, never to revert back to his old self. The self, which at 82, still refused to be old!

The next eight months (after February 2018, that is), I could not write anything. (One or two FB posts, I felt retrospectively, could have been written as a KD post). But it was only from late October 2018 that I started to write this blog seriously.

15 months into my return, I had realized that my new life would give me NO TIME for writing. But if I could not write at least 500-1000 words a week, I would die! So, I settled, initially, for one post per week. I did that for 5 weeks in a row, late-October to late-November, gritting my teeth. However, it was also something apart from determination that made it happen: I got to breathe for the first time in three months after joining a new University as the Head of a Department.

Since then, I have been writing, on average, twice a month. Though there have been months I have not written at all, while in some others I wrote as many as four posts; once, in June 2019, I pulled off a memorable hat-trick, writing three posts in three days in a row!

Blogging the personal

I have been blogging since 2014. I first started blogging about films (Hindi and Bengali cinema), and then gravitated towards writing about my personal life ('Life in the Netherlands') in early 2016 – which I continued for about a year (February 2016 to March 2017). It would be another year before I commenced with 'Kolkata Diaries'. While both are blogs about my personal life, there is an important difference between them.

My life in NL was what it was. Kolkata came in, for sure, in the posts I wrote then. (How can one escape or forget the past?) But my life there had a rhythm of its own, that was primarily grounded in the present. When I started writing the blog, I had been living there for almost a decade, and my life had developed its own memory in that place. But 'Kolkata Diaries' I started writing after relocating back to India. The 'back' is important. In fact, it is the most important thing here. I had come back to my home city with a child. The memory now was not just that of NL, but of an earlier self in an earlier Calcutta/Kolkata: the city that was no more, whose signs and streets had changed considerably. My 'home', too, had changed irrevocably, with my mother gone, and me settling down in my natal place, 18 years after I had left it (for what I thought was for good).

I have mostly written about the lives that surround - and impinge upon - mine ('Meshomoshai and his New Neices', 'An Aspirational Family'). And, of course, about my daughter ('S's Summer', 'Experiencing Pain at 7'). Being a working mother defines my life at the moment, and I have dealt with that more than my work itself, though the latter also featured sometimes.

Living with a widowed father has opened my eyes to the vulnerabilities of old age in a way I would not have otherwise ('Doctor and Patient', 'ICU Stepdown'). I have paid many tributes: to role models ('Kajaldi'); people I admire ('The New Fotolab'); friends I cherish ('Anna', 'Brototi', 'Runa'). I have also looked back a lot: on special occasions associated with my mother ('My Matrilineal Inheritance', 'Waiting for You', 'Hajar-Buti'); on childhood memories ('Chumki Maima', 'Shyambajar-er

Mashimuni'); my life in Amsterdam ('The Sky above Us', 'Gorom Bhaat').

From late March this year, however, unwittingly, my 'Kolkata Diaries' became more like 'Lockdown Diaries' – as I wrote about my experience of being quarantined at home, totally engrossed in the here and now ('When Home is Not Home', 'Exhausted').

Desperate writing

This blog has been a long, desperate bid to be able to write at all. For the most part, it has varied from 500-1000 words; but there have also been much longer posts, standing anywhere between 1200 to 2000 words. My usual method is to type on my laptop, and once the post is ready after several drafts, to copy-paste the final version on my FB wall. But I have deviated from my usual method very often.

I have written in all manner of places and times: early morning, before class; late night, in a dark bedroom, with a sleeping child beside me, in the faint light that came from the open attached bathroom; in a doctor's clinic, waiting my turn; at Inox, before a show began. (There was also this one blissful instance, when, on a lazy Sunday morning, I typed out a post first thing after the morning tea. It was winter and the sun was soft on my feet, as I lay them out on the cold floor).

These exercises could only be possible with a smartphone: I drafted in my Samsung Notes and then copy-pasted, as usual, on my wall. The accompanying photos were mostly from my phone 'Gallery', so that way, this strategy worked well.

A third – and the most desperate of all strategies – was when I wrote directly on my wall, with the setting, 'Only Me'. These were for posts that I was procrastinating on for way too long. Writing ON the wall ensured that they got written. The remaining process was the same: drafts, and then posting the final version with a photograph (or several of them).

The Facebook posts have been important for me. I am not on Twitter and still figuring things out on Instagram. When I make a submission, in my Bio note, I write: "She writes reviews and features for online portals, and blogs at http://www.royrituparna.com/". But actually, I do not post on my website. Not at first, anyway. I post directly on FB. Because I found out at some point that those that I post directly, people read. But when I give the link to my website, people usually do not. (I have no idea why.) Hence, I have settled for posting first on my FB wall and then updating the post on my website.

Gratitude

I would like to take the opportunity today to thank all those who have read my blog, especially my regular readers. They know who they are! Some of them are among my closest friends, but there are also others whom I have never met in person, and have never shared any phase of my life with. We met on FB, and our relationships have been nurtured primarily on our walls, in the 'Comments' section of our posts. I feel particularly blessed with these connections, because they allow me to reach a wider circle of readers. Their feedback has helped me gauge the overall reception of my blog over 24 months.

I hope they continue reading it!!

ON BEAUTY (1 December 2020)

This is a post in response to one by a friend – which in turn was a response to a photograph of mine that I had posted this morning, which elicited a lot of compliments. I could not share my friend's post, so I am copy-pasting what she wrote here:

"Rituparna's post, where she looks stunning with a new haircut set me thinking. I abjure submitting to the beauty of the body publicly from today. While I was never good-looking to begin with, plus being too tall and dusky for average Bengali liking, I now see the insidiousness behind saying *ki sundor lagche*, o how beautiful you look. It is a lever, men and women have used to debilitate women. Does anyone say *ki sundor lagche* to a man at first sight? Then why should a woman be pulled at her nose by the beauty ring? Being healthy is enough. Even not being healthy is enough! I will throw things at people who say *sundor lagche, kalo lagche, mishti lagche*. Got it????"

✦✦✦

I must say I was surprised that my post prompted/generated another thread of conversation elsewhere. I had no idea it could have this effect! Also, a small correction: I did not have a new haircut – what can be seen now is simply my natural hair growth, after I shaved it off six weeks back.

To come to what my friend said, first, I would like to thank her for calling out a practice that dehumanizes women while apparently trying to praise them. As she presciently points out: "I now see the insidiousness behind saying ki *sundor lagche*, o how beautiful you look. It is a lever, men and women have used to debilitate women". I could not agree more with her – that, historically, women have always been reduced to their bodies (and wombs); and that this pernicious habit continues even into this day and age.

Seen carefully, her post deals with two inter-related aspects of the problem: body-shaming, which has to do with acceptable parameters of beauty; and the conflation of physical appearance with one's overall personality and being.

I would like to share my own experience of some of these aspects. But I would also like to problematize the discussion by differentiating between the mindless praise of physical beauty and the appreciation of beauty as part of the aesthetic experience of life.

✦✦✦

My friend was disliked, she says, for being tall and dusky, as that did not fit the bill of a Bengali girl. I have seen the same logic being applied in my own family for three generations – with my mother, sister and daughter.

My mother was spoken of, in the most derogatory of tones, by her in-laws as 'bete-mota' (short and fat). Yes, she had put on weight after four operations within a few years of marriage and was less than the Bengali female average in height. But she also had the other parameters of a traditional Bengali beauty: fair complexion and a beautiful face, and those who loved her always praised those. (Of course, just being fair was good enough, for many of them, because for the longest time, the formula was: fair = beautiful). Ma's firstborn, my sister, suffered – right from childhood through adolescence to youth – for her complexion. It would now be called 'dusky' (after its association with supermodels since the 90s), but back in the 70s and 80s, it was termed 'dark'. She was a 'kalo meye'. Period. All her qualities somehow came after that. It hugely affected her self-esteem when she was growing up and it would take her years to shake it off. A generation later, I faced another version of this with my daughter. She was born in Amsterdam, a South-Asian diasporic child (of Bengali-Bihari descent) in a white European nation. It was intriguing to see how differently people reacted to her complexion: while my Dutch friends drooled over her dusky skin, the 'tan' they spent a lot of money to acquire on distant beaches, a lot of my Indian acquaintances would remark on the fact that she did not get my complexion. She won everyone with her smile, though!

Maybe I had all of this at the back of my mind when I chose to have a dusky female protagonist for a novel I began writing in 2015 (shelved for several years now). It was set in the late 80s, when she is in college and has a long-distance relationship, which is what the story is about. But her struggles with her complexion are a part of it.

✦✦✦

I have never shied away from praising beauty, never not liked being praised for it. I have never shied away from complimenting men, either: from qualities I admire in them to looks and attire but I have certainly always disliked anyone being reduced to just that.

I am innately feminine. Most of the stereotypes that women have had to fight against (because they do not fit this or that description) come naturally to me: I like clothes and jewellery and cosmetics, I have always wanted to marry and have a child, and I love domesticity. You name it. Except for cooking, which I have never liked – but I ended up doing a lot of even that for a decade! While I did not have to struggle with these stereotypes, there were other, more subtle ones I contended with: that being feminine was somehow tantamount to not being ambitious, that one could not desire family life and aspire for one's place in the world with equal intensity. Another even more subtle one was – being an academic meant you had to look/dress/behave 'intellectual'. Even socialize intellectually! I have been gloriously unfit in these other respects.

What I am trying to get at is that stereotypes operate not just with respect to gender, but in all spheres of life – all of which entail reducing a human being to a set of assumptions. And if we can use 'looks' as a synonym for 'beauty' (inadequate though it is, no doubt), then we will realize how superficial our responses are to a lot of the things we do not pay attention to.

I personally associate beauty with aesthetics. Growing up, I imbibed a certain aesthetic sense from my mother, in whom I saw it operate in everything she did: the way she kept house, dressed, and wrote poetry. So, when I first encountered Keats' famous lines in college – "A thing of beauty is a joy forever" – I did not restrict its provenance to only the literary or artistic appreciation of beauty. In the succeeding decades, I have only learnt to recognize and appreciate more beauty all around me – in nature and the elements, in architecture, in the maddening variety of things and objects that make up our daily life, in colour and form, rhythm and sound, thought and expression, people and relationships. And yes, the human body. If anything, my admiration for it has increased infinitely more after the birth of my child and seeing her grow.

GOLDEN JUBILEE (3 December 2020)

This adorable pair are my parents, pictured soon after their wedding.

Today, 3rd December 2020, marks the 50th marriage anniversary of my parents – their golden jubilee! I am supposed to feel sad that Ma is not around to celebrate it (she left us four years back) … but I am not. In fact, I am relieved she is not here. Like every 3rd December since 2016, I feel happy that life has spared her yet another hollow anniversary.

She usually looked her saddest on this day, and Baba clueless. Their anniversary was a celebration that we forced on them. More specifically, I forced on them… and didi tagged along. Like everything else in their marital life, they did this one, too, for us: giving in to an annual ritual, to give us joy. But like all forced things, it lacked soul and was always quickly gotten over and done with.

✦✦✦

In social gatherings, I remember, they always looked good together. They were the pride of their families and were respected as a 'Professor couple' (never mind that she left her service soon after marriage). He was widely admired for his idealism, she for her sacrifices. They did all they could for their families – Baba all along; Ma before marriage and haltingly, after it. And they gave us, their children, a decent life – a genteel, middle-class one – in a nice apartment complex situated in a pleasant neighbourhood of a cosmopolitan city. We studied in good institutions, tried to make something of our lives. Their story is supposed to be simply a summation of these duties: what they did as children and siblings, and how they fared as parents. But it is not. They were a couple first – even if the society they lived in (or is it just the circles they moved in?) never acknowledged it.

Buried under their 'genteel', 'decent' exterior were a plethora of silences and resentments, deep hurts and betrayals. And sometimes, merciless fights and arguments. The disconnect between them was exposed in those. A lot of it had to do with Baba's financial indiscretions – too much money spent on worthy causes, unworthy people – the onus of which had to be borne by Ma. (Baba not only spent a fortune in a protracted legal battle he was engaged in at his college and for which Ma pawned her jewellery, he also incurred heavy losses in a partnership business of electronic goods he had with three friends – which he made good by giving ALL the money he got from selling his share of the family property. Not an *anna* came to his home). While Ma stood by Baba in most of his ventures, growing anxieties about the future of the two daughters with almost no savings took a toll on her health. It is this anxiety – of the lack of adequate money where there should not have been any, and the consequent fear of a bleak future – that defined our family life.

But the lack of money was not the whole story. The lack of love was even more pronounced. Each generation has its own ideas of love and how to express it, and its own ways to measure the lack thereof. Some of it is transmitted to the children. So, it was with Ma and us. We sensed a sorrow in her – that was partly the remnants of a fatherless existence… but also something else. It was in our adolescence, and especially young adulthood, that we could crack the code: when we became keenly aware of the love Ma longed for and that Baba was incapable of giving. We thus grew up unwittingly imbibing the pain of that gap between yearning and fulfilment, and in time, didi and I would each arrive at our own theories about it, would each strive to change that fate for ourselves with a different formula.

Old age – that dream of a beatific long walk into the sunset, holding hands, that is peddled in advertisements of everything from insurance plans and old-age homes to biscuits and jewellery – did not change anything for Baba-Ma. Life only got more difficult – in itself, and with each other. The social obligations were reduced, but there were disappointments galore from the children. And only each other's failing health for company. Ma's death brought an end to that.

✦✦✦

Marriage was a long truancy for Baba and for Ma, a long punishment: as I look back, that is how I see it. But I say this without any rancour. For a long time, I could not forgive Baba for not being the husband I would have liked him to be; my sympathies lay totally with Ma. But I have revised that opinion in later years, as I came to admire him more and more as an individual and came to understand the essentially binary nature of the things he pursued, with that of a routine domestic life. As to the laws of love and attraction, I now understand they are beyond the pale of reason. And more often than is admitted, people find both outside of marriage. Whatever he was as a husband, Baba was always a loving father, even when he gave us very little time. And post-retirement, he became invested in our lives and careers in a way that we had not imagined possible. We thus learnt to appreciate him more as a parent later in life.

But this post is not about Baba-Ma as parents, but of them as a couple. And I am incapable, any more, of celebrating any couple, any relationship, which has had very little going for itself – beyond an accumulated mass of expectations and duties. That is the norm; that is the model of marriage that has the widest acceptance, I know. I only refuse to celebrate that model. And thereby endorse, and help perpetuate, its damaging afterlives.

Both Baba and Ma married because their families wanted them to. Baba was already set in his bachelor ways in 1970 and could have easily remained gloriously single all his life. Ma could not have easily achieved that… but she could certainly have had a better marriage, one that did not deplete her so completely. But it is useless to speculate now…

I am grateful, though, that they came together – didi and I would not have happened otherwise. I am even more grateful that Ma chose to keep me, even when her gynaecologist had advised her against it. By defying him, she gave me the gift of a life, and didi, a sibling. That is all we sisters have: each other. In our middle age now, we realize this more than ever before!

✦✦✦

Meanwhile, here they are in this faded photograph, Kalpana and Biren – young, beautiful, looking the perfect new couple. I want to hug them together, an arm around each neck. I love them so…

NITA and SHANKAR (10 January 2021)

Is it possible to die again after one's death? I believe it is. For, does not one die a little more with each loved one joining the ranks of the dead? With each death, does not one lose one more trace among the living … till none is left at all?

My mother died again last week, when her elder brother – the dearest person in her life, and certainly the man she loved the most – passed away on 3rd January.

Boro Mama's (that is what we call our eldest maternal uncle in Bangla) passing was actually a blessing – for him, more than anyone else. For he had been struck with paralysis after an accident in 2001 and could never recover the autonomy of his body in the two decades since. It is the kind of curse that none would wish on others, even when one is tended to by a devoted wife as he was, and had other blessings in the form of children and grandchildren as he did.

✦✦✦

Mama's death has brought with it a flood of memories for me… all of them of childhood. One of the things I distinctly remember is that, while growing up, more than Boro Mama, we were drawn to Mejo Mama – Ma's younger brother – who would visit us on Sundays, invariably with Eclairs hidden in his trouser-pockets, two each for didi and me. How we waited for that! Also, for the sheer delight of his company: he would crack jokes, make fun of every family member (including himself), update Ma with the latest sibling-news (they were three brothers and four sisters), and relish the snack she quickly made for him, all the while asking her not to bother but sit down and chat.

Boro mama did not have it in him to delight children. He would quiz us on history, ask us difficult questions about school, and then usually hold forth on the policies of the Left Front government. The latter he engaged in mostly with Baba, whose opinion he valued and whom he regarded with the utmost respect. That respect was, in fact, mutual.

Baba had profound admiration for Mama for taking on the responsibility of an entire family when their father had died suddenly, leaving them destitute. Mama had to transform himself into the man of the house, overnight, then.

"From being forced into manual labour at the age of fourteen to the time he became a factory worker at Philips at eighteen, he was driven by a single purpose – he had to fend for his family and bring it close to at least a semblance of 'normalcy'. He was more a father than a brother to his siblings and was adored and loved by them unreservedly. But he himself thought little of the herculean responsibility that he had shouldered from such a tender age. Instead, it was his sister's achievements that he was immensely proud of".

I put the last paragraph within quotes, because that is from a story in my maiden collection of shorts, *Gariahat Junction*. That story – 'A Wasted Dream' – is about Ma, and it focuses on her early marital relationship with Baba when she had a traumatic experience. Mama is only part of her back story.

In her maiden life, though, he was central to her existence. After all, they were comrades in a very long battle against poverty. There was something sacred about the closeness of this bond – of the solidarity of having struggled together for a common goal – that never changed. It was also a kind of 'partnership' that could not be replicated in their later lives with their spouses.

✦✦✦

We had heard stories of Boro Mama and Ma's struggles pretty early in our childhood. And we also witnessed for ourselves how special they were to each other. I interpreted this as them being each other's 'favourite' sibling. But I understood the nature of their bond much later in life – when I first saw Ritwik Ghatak's film *Meghe Dhaka Tara* (1960, the first of his Partition trilogy). With Ma, of course. When I saw her silently cry throughout the film, I could immediately see the connection with her life. It was not so much a resonance as resemblance – to a very great extent.

In Ghatak's classic, Nita, a young East-Bengali refugee woman living in a colony in Calcutta, struggles to maintain her impoverished family by giving up on her own dreams. She is exploited by those closest to her, does not get to marry, and dies of TB. While her beloved elder brother, Shankar - whose talent she believes in and supports unconditionally - ironically achieves recognition as a singer just as her days end.

My mother did not face the kind of rank familial exploitation that Nita did. She also got to marry (though at a time she was not prepared for it) when the family saw better times. Her elder brother, too, was no famous artist, but a humble cog in a giant corporate wheel, who remained so all his life. They were not refugees living in a colony, either. But despite these obvious differences, they struggled similarly, and in the same historical time, the 1950/60s. Their partnership was vital for the survival of their family.

Meghe Dhaka Tara is one of my all-time favourites. And I can never watch Nita and Shankar without thinking of Ma and Boro Mama, the Nikhil and Kabita of my story.

Mama's name was 'Nirmal' – which means pure. He was just that. May he rest in peace.

MISSING S! (18 May 2021)

HAPPY MOTHERS DAY

> Dear mama,
> I am very grateful for who you have made me. You have made me a great child, and helped me get through many situations. I have learned so much from you and I need to learn so much more. You and I have gone through so much together, and I really hope that we can get over covid.

I miss S!

It's been exactly three weeks since she's been away from me, staying with her dad and his parents. And it will be almost another two before she can return. A whole month (or more)!

Reason? I tested Covid positive three weeks back and got admitted to a nursing home the day after – thanks to my wonderful doctor-friend, Saurabh Basu. I returned after twelve days. But just two days later, my father tested positive. Thankfully, he is asymptomatic and quarantining at home. But he is very fragile, given his age. And his quarantine means I will have to wait for a longer time before S can return.

*****

This is our longest separation in all her nine years. May it never exceed this span, I earnestly hope… till she flies the nest! Which is another nine years away (only nine?!) … assuming she will leave after high school.

My head has been full of these numbers and calculations – of weeks, months, years. But what I have missed most all this while is her touch. I had rediscovered touch after she was born, and my love for her ever since has been wholly tactile. How else can one love a child?

Loving a baby is all about loving the baby's body – nursing, bathing, cleaning, soothing. Everything has to do with touch. While sound and sight are important, it is primarily touch that connects a baby to her mother. As she grows to toddler and then child, the hours of contact with the mother steadily decrease, but the importance of touch in the bond remains just the same. And for those who sleep together, it can never be overestimated.

S has slept with me ever since she left her cot (which was placed on my side of our bed, by the way, and not in a different room). She has never slept alone in a room: we have, thus, always begun and ended our days together. She is the first thing I see in the morning and telling stories (or talking about 'stuff') is the last thing we do at night. I call her my 'kol-balish' (side-pillow); though, in reality, it is mostly her legs which are on me. Throughout the night, she turns 180 degrees in bed several times, but whichever angle she is at, at any given moment, she somehow manages to have at least one leg over me – over my thigh, waist, back, tummy, you name it. It is difficult to fathom sometimes whether she is sleeping or doing stretching exercises, with me as a prop. She also, very often, as good as pushes me out of the bed. "Shar-er moto gutosh na to amae", I shout out involuntarily, breaking my own sleep–for that is exactly what she does, lean into my back with her head, like a bull with his horns. But there are sweet moments, too; the sweetest being, when she curls up into my torso, in an almost foetal position. I wrap my arms around her – this time, deepening my sleep!

✦✦✦

Why am I going on and on about sleeping? That is because sleep time is the only time of ours together that was not compromised in the past 14 months. The first 6/7 months of work from home last year were cruel, as full-time professional work had to be balanced with domestic work without any help, and S's routine. To that was added my father's increasingly fragile health, which had to be attended to – with the result that I could give very little time to S, outside of monitoring her online classes and helping with her homework sometimes. We did get to lunch together - the real gift of work from home - but weekday lunches were often very hurried affairs for me, as I had classes after it.

It was very ironic: pre-pandemic, because of long hours at my workplace, I had never been able to give her much time during the week, but during the pandemic, even working from home could not change that. Even then, I had very little time for her. Meanwhile, Baba seemed to age some three years in six months, and November onwards, I had no alternative but to keep a full-time, live-in attendant for him. This was a first for him and us. In the next four months, three such attendants would come and go, even as his health deteriorated beyond imagination. I found myself totally taken up with this: calling up ayah-centres incessantly, talking to possible candidates over the phone/in person, settling them down with their routines with Baba, trying to get the two adjusted to each other (which was the toughest part) … and when they left, repeating the exercise!

November to January was one story; from February, it became quite another. Because from 1st February, we were required to take online classes from our campus; and that meant I was away for 10 hours, with an 8-year-old child and an 86-year-old sick father at home, at the mercy of unreliable help. I remote-controlled whatever I could, calling up several times a day between classes. From March, I got a reliable help; but from April, Baba became totally bed-ridden, even as dementia set in. This necessitated an additional night attendant for him. The first left after four days of work, the second after a week, and then the first came back again. I am hoping she will stay, and the current pair will become a stable one. That would be heaven!

Needless to say, all of this affected my time with S. It has been tough for her this past year… but she has coped with it remarkably well. I am so amazed by that!

✦✦✦

In my 12 days in the nursing home - when time did not seem to move - I missed her terribly. When we video-called, I would plant famished kisses on the phone screen, instead of blowing a kiss while saying 'bye'. She was faintly amused by my desperation then. Not so now. For one, I have stopped acting silly: I kiss her by touching her face with my fingertips and then placing them on my lips – social distancing even over the phone. She grins from ear to ear when I do that. For her part, her kiss is incomplete without her uttering 'muaah'.

We do not talk a lot - I am simply incapable of that now - but we both wait for the evening video-call. (That is the fixed one; a second may or may not happen during the day or night). We exchange the day's updates. From what I hear, I understand that, apart from keeping up with her drawing, she is basically lazing, and that what she enjoys most is meditating with her dad – though that is a very small part of her day. She has also just got his Tintin collection – I have given her a reading challenge of finishing it before she returns. Hope that peps her up!

She does need pepping up. She sounded listless the last few days. Sometimes she is very quiet, with moments of complete silence… I always break that with "I miss you, beta". It is like the refrain of a song that I just cannot help singing. She is less forthcoming about her feelings. But today she said, "I miss you so much, Mamma. And I just wish sometimes I could hold you tight". I cried. When will I ever be dignified in love?

During those 12 days in the nursing home, in a small room that sealed me off from the world, a video would play in my mind, with a lovely background score. In it, images of us would slide by: S and me lazing in the winter sun on our window sill; reading a book together on the couch, her left arm linked into my right, her head nestled on my shoulder; of freshly bathed S, smelling of flowers, suddenly hugging me round the waist and burying her head in my chest as I dry her wet hair with a towel; of her counting stars in the balcony, sitting on my lap; of her curling up into my torso during sleep.

✦✦✦

I have waited to write this post; I wanted to come at least to the end of my period of isolation at home before writing it. But I have also hesitated writing it – or rather, posting it. It is too self-indulgent. At a time when people are dying like flies everywhere and entire families are being wiped out, it is a luxury to talk of missing a child on the other side of the city. My heart goes out to the bereaved families; I know many myself. But this is my reality, this is what I feel; and this is what the crux of my experience of Covid has been, emotionally – missing my child! I cannot ignore or obliterate that.

Of what it has been for me, in medical and physical terms, is a different story. I feel very grateful that I got a bed and medical care when it was required. And though my recovery phase has been mostly taken up with dealing with Baba's Covid, even as I gear up to resume teaching online later in the week, I just hope that my still low energy levels improve eventually. And that Baba, too, recovers by the end of this month!

Meanwhile, I am counting days for S's return…

A TINY PROTRUSION (16 July 2021)

I have a slight protrusion in the middle finger of my right hand, just below the rim of the nail, on the left side of the finger. It used to be a solid, tiny ball of swollen flesh once, with distended skin, abrasive to the touch: a gift from Exams taken 25/30 years ago.

Those were the most defining Exams of my life – Higher Secondary, Honours and Masters. HS was the toughest of all, as it entailed writing two three-hour papers on a single day. Every day. Yes, 6 hours of writing, with a 1-hour break between the two papers – in which I gulped down small tetra packs of Frooti, or a *daab* (coconut water), while hurriedly going through notes a final time, with Baba persuading me (mostly unsuccessfully) to have some food.

Exams days were his duty: he would take me, hair dripping with oil and a curd-dot on my forehead, to the Exam centre and then back home in a taxi and stuff me with goodies all the way. He was least interested in knowing how the Exam went, his chief concern being how much food and drink I have had during the day and that I should commute comfortably – 'aram kore' - after having conquered the world with my answer scripts.

The same ritual - from the 6 hours of writing to the Frooti and taxi-rides - was repeated for my BA Pass Exams, two years later. The Honors and MA Exams had 4-hour Papers. Since my subject was English Literature, there was a lot to write, and the 4 hours always seemed not enough time to write it in. In fact, while I wanted to shine in every paper, I secretly wished to have at least one question in each that I did not know well… so that I would have a little less to write for one answer! Knowing all equally well would either mean (a) not being able to finish the paper, or worse, (b) finishing in a hurry, unable to 'show off' in the answer! This was also the case with the 3+3 hours Papers (as all Arts subjects asked questions that necessitated descriptive answers).

For half a decade, my life was defined by the inevitability of those annual Exams, a whole year of myriad academic activities invariably leading up to a few days or weeks of gruelling Exams, the cruellest part of which was writing tomes within 3/4 hours. The brunt of that pressure, quite literally, was borne by the middle finger of the right hand. Because, while the pen was held between the forefinger and thumb, the pressure of the instrument actually fell on the middle finger – just under the rim of the nail, on its left side. Pushing the pen vigorously and fast against it, for hours, over days, pushed the flesh of that tiny area up into a protrusion. It used to pain a lot then, the area bulging a wee bit more with every successive Exam, the pain freshly renewed each time. Over the period of the next two decades, however, the bulge would decrease, but never quite go away, nor would the abrasiveness of the skin soften.

✦✦✦

I found myself involuntarily touching that bulge repeatedly today, after the bombshell that Calcutta University dropped on us last night, and enraged posts from students and teachers alike poured out in social media about the insanity of preponed Exams in an already much-reduced Semester and the inhumanity of thrusting 6-hour Exam days on students.

I am myself most concerned about the preponement. The 6-hour Exams are not new to CU, as I have just recounted, but we need to remember that this current schedule is far worse than what we faced – because the students will also have to scan and upload their papers (a panic-stricken exercise for all concerned, given the number of things that might go wrong) in the one-hour break they will have, thus considerably reducing their time to eat and take a breather. At the end of 3 hours of incessant writing and racing against time, fingers usually go numb; it is a torture to go through the hurried scanning process anyway after that; to do it twice over in a single day is to wilfully increase that torture.

I carry the tiny bulge like a tattoo on my finger – a lifelong reminder of years of toil and aspiration, tinged with the hope of a bright future. Of merit rewarded.

My students, too, have the same aspirations; I know. Can we please stop playing with their future?

THE MARK ON THE WALL (June 2020)

A tall child

I first marked her height on our bedroom wall in March 2018, eight months after we returned to India. She was seven weeks short of six years then. She was hugely excited by this exercise: standing at 3 feet 9 inches as she did, it proved to her, she was a tall girl. She was indeed tall among her class/batch mates, looking especially so on the days I brushed back and tied up her hair in a bun – a single ponytail folded in, to keep her shoulders free.

She was tall not only in her new school in Kolkata, but also at the international school she went to in Amsterdam. She could only attend kindergarten there. It was the same in her two-and-a-half years of playschool as well. In fact, right from the time she was a baby, she was relatively tall; I was even told she was always a bit more than the Dutch average in height at any given point of time. That was news!

I never measured her height in Amsterdam. The OKC ('Ouder en Kind Centrum', or Parent-Child Centre/Baby Clinic) did that regularly for us: from age 0-4, in growth record books that changed their cover-colour every year. In her fifth year, I refrained from doing it. But close to her sixth in India, I marked out her height on the bedroom wall.

Moving back home

That bedroom was my bedroom for 21 years, which I had shared with didi (my elder sister). I now share it with S. Most of the furniture of that room has remained the same for over (or nearly)

40 years; the 'new' dressing table that I had gifted Ma after getting a full-time job is also sixteen years old now. I sleep on the same bed, still have the same study table (though I hardly study there anymore), and use the same attached bath and balcony that I did while growing up in this flat. Only, didi has been replaced by S. She is both my future and my past. In her, I live my childhood daily – in numerous ways, big and small.

A lot of women bring their child/children up in the same city where they grew, or may even spend long spells with them in their natal home (after giving birth, during vacations, family functions, emergencies), but few bring them up in the same home. *I* never thought I would. After all, S was born five years after we had relocated to Amsterdam, and her own first five years were also spent there. We were well settled in the Netherlands and I thought we would continue. But life has a way of springing surprises....

I have been living with my child in the home I grew up in for close to three years now. But the person who symbolized home for me is gone – Ma. Coming back to a Ma-less Kolkata has been painful, but *living in* a Ma-less home defies description. The strangeness of it has worn off now, somewhat (though it re-visits me in sudden moments every now and then) ... and I am more or less resigned to my fate, especially after the pandemic hit us in March 2020. As I go about my life in this flat, I often find myself doing things Ma did, in the way she did them. I have, however, resisted one thing – marking S's height on the wall, the way Ma did ours, regularly.

One day in March 2018, however, I was struck by how much S seemed to have grown since our return; and on a whim, I marked her height – a pencil mark against the blue paint of the bedroom wall, on its right side, in the portion that is always hidden behind the door. But I kept delaying the repeat exercise in 2019. I often keep delaying things for an odd variety of reasons; some get delayed, inevitably, in a routine, busy life, but this was different. It had nothing to do with a busy life or forgetfulness or whimsicality.

Anne Frank Huis, Amsterdam

Freaky - and downright unbelievable - as it might sound, what kept me from the repeat exercise was a memory from the Anne Frank House in Amsterdam.

I had read *The Diary of Anne Frank* when I was in Class VIII. It was my first introduction to the Holocaust. But I do not think I understood the full implications of the story, even after what I read in the 'Introduction' and the 'Foreword' of the book. That this story was a part of the bigger story of the annihilation of Jews during World War II, a prelude to the gas chambers in Auschwitz, Bergen-Belsen and a dozen other places in East Europe, did not quite sink in. It would later, in my university years, as I took an interest in the history of that time, and especially after seeing *Schindler's List*. The full horror of it I would wake up to only in 2007, when I first visited Berlin and stopped at the open 'Memorial to the Murdered Jews of Europe', designed by Peter Eisenman, during a walking tour; and in an even more visceral way, in 2016, when I made a research trip to Berlin to study the Holocaust Memorials there, and got to visit Jewish Museum Berlin, Topography of Terror and Museum Sachsenhausen just outside the city. Back in the late 1980s, though, as a mere 13-year-old, I could mostly relate to the 'diary' of a girl my age. She was not only my age; she also did what I loved doing most – record her daily life in a diary. Furthermore, she wanted to be a journalist or writer – just the thing I dreamt of at that point. And she had a whole lot of feelings that I did at the time. I was thus saddened when her life in the Secret Annexe was disrupted and her family was forcefully taken away. But what stayed with me long after I had finished the book was her experiences in that 'Acherhuis' at Prinsengracht 263, for three years, not the sudden termination of it in 1944.

I thus took an early opportunity to visit the Anne Frank Huis after my relocation to Amsterdam in 2007. What left the greatest impression on me in that visit were some marks on the wall: Anne's mother would mark the heights of her daughters during the years of their hiding – those remained in the museum that the house got transformed into. All the paraphernalia and memorabilia related to the years of hiding of the Franks in the Achterhuis, all that is recorded in the 'Diary', find a place in the museum. But it was the relatively innocuous marks on the wall that left the greatest mark upon me. I had goose bumps seeing them, and could not resist my tears.

The effect they had on me probably had something to do with my own growing-up years. They resonated with my childhood (though in a different continent, in another time): a mother marking the height of her daughters; measuring out the progress of time, of developmental growth, through them; seeing in those marks the childhood that is gradually, inevitably lost and maturity gained.

Ever since my visit to the Anne Frank Huis, I have had an eerie feeling about a mark on the wall that records height/growth. I know that that eager, diligent exercise by a proactive mother can turn to ashes, the growth suddenly stopped, life giving way to death. A happy ritual can turn into an ill omen, a tragic irony at best.

I could never rid my mind of this association, hence my reluctance to mark S's height on the wall. I know this sounds weird, but it is true!

Away from Mimi

I had marked S soon after her 'Mimi', my sister, had left in 2018, after a protracted four-month visit. We will never forget those four months.

Didi had come home for a three-week holiday in December 2017. Halfway through it, she had an accident and had to undergo knee surgery in early January 2018, which prolonged her stay till mid-February. But before she could leave, Baba almost lost his life with a freak kidney failure that kept him in the ICU for five weeks – hence, she had to further extend her stay till the end of March. Her three weeks became four months – mostly hospital months. What it gave us - apart from the endless uncertainties and anxieties - was time together. After almost 20 years, since that time when we sisters had both left home for different reasons.

The best part of those four months was, however, not us, but the time that S got to spend with her Mimi, inadvertently – loads of extra fun-time, when a lot was accomplished playfully: learning Bengali, straitening crooked English alphabets, practicing tables, and impromptu dancing every half a chance they got. All of it liberally peppered with quite a bit of scolding and crying and arguing as well… and then making up frantically with hugs and kisses. (Ma must have been delighted to see the antics of these two from wherever she was watching us)!

We knew that didi would not be able to come that Christmas, as she is wont to, as she had used up all her holidays, had in fact to take extraordinary leave. But we were hoping to see her in 2019 – either in the summer, autumn (during Durga Puja) or winter (during the Christmas break, this was most likely). We would meet after more than a year; that much we knew. But that we would not meet at all in 2019, we had not guessed.

It is now more than two years since we have not seen her, and I, for one, am a little sick of the video-chats; sick of digital intimacy. Her problem is a different one: since video-conferencing is a way of life with her as an IT professional, and has been for a long time, she is not jittery about it at all; however, she continuously frets about the fact that she is missing out on S's growing-up years. She loves her niece in that special way unique to aunts; hence, I totally get her restlessness in this matter.

Didi is indeed missing out on a lot. This April, on 'Poila-Baisakh' (the Bengali New Year), S insisted that I mark her height again. I was reluctant, but I could not tell her the reason. With the outbreak of the pandemic, the mark on the wall in the Anne

Frank Huis had come to haunt me again. Obviously, the Nazi occupation of the Netherlands and the pandemic we were facing could not be compared, but the forced confined life (which no one knew how long it would continue) and the shadow of death were palpable. In the initial weeks after the pandemic hit us in India, I was absolutely paralyzed with fear: afraid of both my father (aged 84) and especially S (now 8) contracting the disease, as children below the age of 10 and the elderly above 60 were declared to be particularly vulnerable. But I somehow overcame that fear. And I gave in to S's request of marking her height.

She stood 5-and-a-half-inches taller than last time, which was 26 months back. There are some BMI implications that can be derived from this. But what those inches represent, more forcefully, is her growth/maturity in other terms.

Didi had left S in Upper Nursery. She has moved up two grades in Junior School after that. At the basic academic level, this is what happened: she had a slew of new subjects in Grade I and Grade II - Bangla, Social Studies and ICT on the one hand, Music, Drama and Art on the other; and in Grade III (which should have commenced by now but unfortunately cannot), she will start learning a foreign language and enrol in at least two ECA's.

Her temperament and inclinations remain the same, though, as when didi had left her in 2018. She loves to draw most of all, likes Maths, hates English composition and is slow in everything she does. Though I must add that the love has increased, the hatred has lessened and the speed has improved a teeny-whiny bit. I am, however, most taken in with her fluency in both Bangla and (especially) English, which have now totally replaced Dutch.

She still speaks Bangla with an accent, but is comfortable in it enough to argue with her 'Dadu' (my dad) in the language. And sometimes stumps me with very long sentences in English with no mistakes in them. Of late, it is not so much the length as *what* she says that takes me by surprise. One day, for instance, when I gave her the cello tape that she was looking for but could not find in her desk, she said: "Thank you very much for taking care of my supplies". She did not look at me while saying it, just walked out of the room, throwing that statement casually behind her. Another day, when I told her I was tired of her ever-ready-to-fall tears whenever I take away my phone from her, she shut me up with a dramatic: "I have emotions, Mamma"!

Locked-down

Emotions, she does have aplenty. Sometimes, she pens it down, like she did during 'Lockdown 1.0' (that started on 23rd March):

"Dear Corona Virus,

I would like you to get out of earth and travel to Mars, it is lovely there, nobody is there, and nobody will try to harm you. If you stay here, I will beat you! And squish you and kill you. If you don't want that to happen then you better get lost from here.

Angry regards from S".

When she insisted that I mark her height on 15th April, we were about to enter 'Lockdown 2.0' (lasting till 3rd May), which eventually got extended to 'Lockdown 3.0' (till 17th May). This one-month (mid-April to mid-May) was a very active month for S, thanks to her Zoom (later, Google Meet) classes, thrice a week

– on Mondays, Wednesdays and Fridays. On each of those days, she would have two regular 40-minute classes in the morning, with a small break in between. Though her teachers had ensured that they had enough work to do at home from the time all the schools closed in mid-March, the online classes were obviously far more enjoyable for the kids. S looked forward to them with great excitement, and with some nudging from me, also managed to submit her many assignments on time. She was a bit sad on the day of her last class, saying she would miss her class teacher, but in the same breath, also added: "I cannot wait to be in Grade III"! Though it was slated to begin only on 10th June, the anticipation of going to school was somehow punctured when 'Lockdown 4.0' (till end-May) was announced. That day, she asked me point-blank: "Will this lockdown never end"?

'Lockdown 4.0' brought with it the devastation of cyclone 'Amphan' to Bangladesh and the states of West Bengal and Odisha in India. Kolkata, too, faced its onslaught. We were actually better off than most others in the city - having had water supply and electricity throughout - but our landline, internet and TV were not working. Of these, the lack of TV was the cruellest blow to S: not being able to spend time with her besties Peppa, Dora, Masha, Shimmer and Shine was unimaginable for her. She also felt betrayed, like thousands of other privileged kids, by the sudden vanishing of the alternate digital universe that they had been encouraged to take for granted after their schools closed.

Unlocked, unsavoury reality

The 'Unlockdown 1.0', since June 1st, is proving to be cruel to S in a wholly different way, for it has brought to the clear light of day the reality that she has suspected for quite a while now – the total lack of physical companionship in her confined life, except for her mother. (Her Dadu is also present at home, of course, but he operates more or less in the background of S's life – there is fondness and affection for each other, but hardly any active engagement between them). The socializing that is a given of S's daily life - with her teachers and friends in school - had already stopped since 16th March. From just a week later, the other giver of her life - the 'aunties' at home - was also lost. She is used to spending a substantial part of her day with her nanny, whom she calls her 'taking care aunty'; her 'cooking aunty' and 'cleaning aunty' complete the triad of domestics at home who make my working life outside it possible. S is fond of all of them and enjoys time spent with them (however varied the time-span with each). They daily commute mostly by train to come and work for us: with the lockdown, that stopped. And it will be quite some time before it can be resumed.

S also spends the weekends with her dad and his parents on the other side of town, and a mid-week evening with him at home. Not being able to do that was the most difficult part of the first two months of lockdown. It was strange to be in the same city and not be able to meet! Daily video-chats in the evenings were only a partial and poor compensation for the real thing.

Thankfully, the situation has changed somewhat since 17th May, and her dad is now visiting her on Saturday afternoons, right after her online ballet lessons. We had missed out on her Birthday celebration in early May this year, our ritual of dining out that evening: on her dad's first visit after the gap, I replaced that with a pasta and pudding lunch at home.

S eagerly looks forward to the Saturday visits; for the rest of the week, she is continuing with her daily video-chats with him, and weekly/bi-weekly ones with her Mimi. But her most engaged conversations are with her 'pretend friends' (even more than with her 'real' friends): they are an amalgamation of her TV besties and her favourite Disney characters (Elsa and Anna, from *Frozen*, and Rapunzel). She spends an awful amount of time with them: there are officially designated periods, throughout the day, for talking with them – on the balcony (when it is punctuated with admiring the newest cat in our building and her kittens), the bedroom or the living room. I remarked the other day that her pretend friends were becoming an obsession with her, to which pat came the reply: "Who else do I talk to, then"? She was not angry or upset when she said that; it was simply a factual statement… that broke my heart.

But I checked myself from feeling guilty. I am not solely responsible for the situation S/we are in, in Kolkata – both before and after Corona; and the fact that I have little time to sit and chat with her is also not my doing. In 'normal' times, I cannot give her the time she wants/needs from me (working days, I hardly get her and on weekends, she is not there); stuck at home now, I am still unable to give her that time, after all the housework, in addition to 'work from home' and my other preoccupations. The toll it has taken on me these last three months is something I cannot communicate to her; just as I cannot tell her the pre-history of the mental exhaustion that I have felt for many years now (which is and is not related to her existence). I am waiting for the time when I can… but I fear that my telling will be the end of her childhood.

S has wondered for a long time why we live at my natal home. She knows her Dadu needs her Mamma, which is not untrue. But she has been fed the most palatable half-truth – one that works wonderfully well both for her and for (the nosy Indian) society at large. Somewhere, I know, she guesses the truth… but holds on to the comfort of what she has been told, for all it is worth. She has many friends in school who also live with only their mothers, their fathers away at work in another country. For the time being, she considers herself in that bracket, which, again, is somewhat true; at a daily, functional level, the situations *are* similar. Where they are not… her understanding of *that* is what will catapult her out of childhood.

I want it and do not want it at the same time: I want it partly to stop (half) faking reality and partly to experience the closure I badly need; I do not want it because I am still scared of the pain it will cause her. I have been told that these things cannot be stage-managed, that I should allow it to happen 'organically'. My intellect understands that argument, but I am not sure if it can be entirely left to 'happen'.

I remember a European gay friend of mine, who co-parents a child with a close female friend of his, telling me that he had revealed the uniqueness of their family situation to his daughter when she was six years old. I had marvelled when I had heard that: at his confidence and wisdom, his daughter's maturity, the level of trust he evidently had with his friend, and the society that allowed such a family to exist.

I am no apologist for all things European, but my gay friend's story made the fake heteronormativity of my existence starker - and almost unbearable - by contrast. Back in India, though, keeping up appearances, I realize, is the norm – "for the sake of the child/children", of course. No matter how bad/dysfunctional/loveless/abusive the marriage, it needs to be adhered to at all costs; that philosophy has not changed much in our generation. Sadly, I mostly find regression in the lived lives of women around me, behind the mask of education and employment.

It is tough to stand by a difficult choice in such an overwhelmingly patriarchal-complicit atmosphere. I have faced that for three years now. But the pandemic has taken it to an altogether different level. I had fallen ill last month, out of sheer exhaustion… but somehow dragged myself out of it. Now, I also want to drag myself out of the stagnant position I am in through the period of the pandemic. That will mean having to confront the whole truth with S; to finally address the elephant in the room.

Will I be able to do that? Will she be able to bear? Will there be another mark on our bedroom wall in April 2021? How many inches more will S grow by then? What is the story they will tell? I wonder….

WINDING JOY (July 2021)

We have a new visitor at home this monsoon: a creeper. And it is difficult to convey just how much joy it has brought in our famished lives - my daughter's and mine.

Sixteen months since the pandemic struck us in India, confinement at home is now a way of life – willy-nilly, we have all adapted ourselves to it; my nine-year old, too. To an extent and with a maturity that amazes and saddens me in equal measure: amazes because hers is after all a very tender age; saddens because life is being so unremittingly cruel to them, clipping their wings even as the world seems to be at their fingertips.

My daughter has figured out her own way of dealing best with the confinement – by spending as much time as she possibly can on our balcony. And she seems to continually discover new delights there: "Mamma, come and see something in the balcony, RIGHT NOW", "Mamma, you HAVE TO see this; "Mamma, you WON'T BELIEVE what has happened today"! I get such urgent summons quite often, during breaks in her online classes; after lunch, when she is unwinding; in the evening, when she is most likely to be stargazing; and at night, before she retires to bed. These are the official balcony times for her, but there are unofficial times as well. And there are n number of reasons for which I can be summoned: the tiniest of butterflies resting on a leaf; the mother cat of our building, sunbathing with her litter; a sparrow perched on the railing; clouds floating by, seeming to touch the terrace of the building opposite us, continuously morphing into ever new shapes; rain slashing hard against our balcony; stars at night on a clear sky (this is her absolute favourite, there is nothing she loves more than star gazing); a full moon, resplendent in her white glory.

She was born and spent the first five years of her life in a beautiful, residential neighbourhood of Amsterdam, where nature was an integral part of the surroundings – from tree-lined avenues and parks to canals lining the streets (home to ducks and fleeting birds) and flowers blooming everywhere (especially in spring and summer). Living on a 9th-floor apartment with wide glass windows also afforded an uninterrupted view of the sky. Her next four years in Kolkata have been spent on a first-floor apartment in a housing complex her mother grew up in with her aunt, in one of the better neighbourhoods of the city. While the location is good and safe overall, the building itself is hemmed in by others on all sides, with a former playground now turned into a virtual parking lot. Result: there is far less green here, and of course, no soothing sight of a water body nearby. All you have is a few trees and the small gardens of those living on the ground floor.

We have clung to their beauty during our confinement at home. This monsoon, we were gifted another.

✦✦✦

There it was, suddenly one morning – a creeper!

It was first a tiny tendril, with the smallest of leaves.

We could not believe how small it was – both my daughter and I touched its tender body, with a curl distinct even in that tiniest of editions. Tactility is the first response to a beautiful object: we want to touch the petals of flowers, the fur of pets, the impossible softness of baby cheeks. The small, tender leaf inspired the same affection in us.

The creeper grew – not little by little, but at an accelerated pace, jumping stages almost. It was in a tremendous rush to reach the top. The most interesting aspect of its growth was that its upper part was always dangling in mid-air… till the point came when it finally hung from balcony floor to ceiling in a suggestion of 'S', though never quite managing the full double curves.

We saw small leaves grow large, overlapping one over the other. The lower portion was more crowded. In the upper part, three perfectly heart-shaped leaves stood alone, gloriously separate. After their presence, I cannot think of a red heart anymore and have begun to respond with green hearts in my comments on WhatsApp and Facebook now!

Seeing the creeper at all times of the day and night and observing the changing play of light on it has been such a delight this monsoon! In the clear light of day, it looks pretty, adding a natural decorative touch to the balcony; at night, it is ethereal, in the reflected glow of a bulb from an adjacent building.

But in the rains, the freshness of its huge leaves is a whiplash on the stupor of our lives – the "living and partly living" that we have been doing for a year and a half.

That freshness also stands in stark - almost violent - contrast to the rusty grills, around which the creeper has wound its way to the top.

✦✦✦

Our building happens to be about 45 years old, its inhabitants primarily the elderly, making it a veritable Geriatric Home. With mandatory fresh painting every few years, however, the building has been pretty well maintained (compared to many others from the same decade). The last time it was painted was a couple of years back. While the building still looks okay, overall, the grills and railings have rusted. Our own apartment was painted last, even earlier – in 2012, in honour of my daughter. Ma wanted to welcome her in a freshly painted home when she first visited as a seven-month-old baby. It has not been repainted since. It was still fresh when Ma suddenly left us in August 2016, and after that, there has been no possibility of repeating the exercise, especially in Covid times.

I try to enliven the rooms by changing the curtains and bed sheets frequently. That always helps. The rooms invariably look a little different with every new permutation-combination of the two. But the dining room is a different matter: it was in a really bad shape and I opted for another solution there: I went for wallpaper which could be pasted on in a matter of hours by just two labourers, without disturbing the routine of the house involving a child and an ailing elderly parent.

But the balcony railings are beyond any such quick fix. The creeper changed that!

It added a small ounce of freshness and joy to counter the rust of age and survive a monsoon shadowed by disease and death.

PS:

Two weeks after writing this essay, a second creeper started winding its way up on the other side of our balcony. My daughter promptly posed before the newest arrival!

KANDINSKY MEETS BEETHOVEN (February 2022)

For two weeks in September 2020, I saw my daughter, S, trying out her school art teacher's prompt: attempting Wassily Kandinsky's synesthetic technique of giving shape and colour to music. The piece that was given to them to do this exercise was Beethoven's 'Moonlight Sonata', which she listened to on loop while working. Never mind that most of the drawing happened in quiet afternoons, with bright sunlight illuminating both the artist and her work!

I had seen a few assignments that had invigorated her as much in the previous 18 Covid months. The last I could think of was another art assignment, the previous summer, when they were taught the Pointillist style.

Kandinsky

We watched the video on Kandinsky that her teacher had uploaded for reference twice together. "For Kandinsky, every colour had a feeling, a sensation, and a sound", the narrative explained. The colours corresponded to instruments in his mind: warm red to "trumpets - strong, harsh and ringing"; cool red to the "sad, middle tones of a cello"; green to "the placid middle notes of a violin"; violet to "an English horn, or the deep notes of a wood instrument", such as the bassoon; blue had a wide range - a light blue was "like a flute, a darker blue a cello, darker still, a thunderous double bass and the darkest blue of all, an organ". White and black corresponded not to specific instruments, but silence and pause in music – white had "the harmony of silence"; and black represented "profound and final pauses".

S listened with attention to this section, learnt the names of instruments she had not known before, and the correspondence between sound and colour, as Kandinsky understood and articulated it. But she did not strain herself to remember them, thankfully, concentrating instead on giving her own interpretation of Beethoven's music.

'Moonlight Sonata'

I saw a swirl of shapes in her composition, with a few circles discernible in it and a prominent triangle; also, the predominance of blue. I asked her why.

"Think of the night sky", she said.

"What about the night sky? It's dark..."

"Yes, dark", she interrupted. "But the dark of indigo, not black".

"Were you thinking of Van Gogh's 'Starry Night'?" I asked, thinking back to one of her art lessons last year.

"No, no… I was just thinking of the regular night sky", she clarified.

And then took off.

"Just hearing the name of the music, 'Moonlight Sonata', I thought of the night sky. Of deep, dark blue. Indigo is… deep feelings. And the shapes… the geometric shapes … they are very spontaneous. When you see clouds or stars in the sky, you can make anything out of them. Since I thought I had the freedom, I drew it like that…"

She paused. I knew she was not done; she was just gathering her thoughts and catching her breath, before continuing, as it were, into the next movement of expression. I kept quiet, like I do in these moments, but I marvelled at her attempt to articulate something that is difficult even for an adult.

I love the night sky, Mamma".

This sounded more like a confession. Indeed, there was more to come.

"I love the peace and darkness of the night. It brings a quiet mood. I want to be by myself then. Feel more peaceful to be alone at night. The most special moments, I want to share with you. And the ones lesser than that, I want to share on my own".

In her own way, my little one was expressing the human need for both solitude and company, I thought. But what struck me the most in all that she said was the way she matched colour with feeling: "Indigo is deep feeling".

I realized that she had taken the exercise of giving form and colour to music one step further – corresponding colour to feelings. I decided to explore that further.

The colour of emotions

The next night, in bed, I asked: "So, for you, indigo is the colour of deep feelings?"

"Yup", pat came the reply.

"Deep feelings… as in pain?"

"No, no, pain is red", she sprang up to correct me.

"Oh. And anger?"

"Orange". This, she said, widening her eyes and started laughing. I knew why. We both find each other's anger funny. Her laughter was a reference to that.

"And what colour is excitement?" I continued, my curiosity having now become a game that we were both enjoying.

"Hot pink", she said with a smile.

"Happiness?"

"Yellow and green", she grinned.

"Because they are bright and fresh?"

She nodded her head vigorously.

"Beauty?"

"White and aqua and teal".

"They are very different colours, beta", I could not help saying.

"Yes… but... they are all… beautiful"!

We both laughed out loud at this – at the limits of expression. It was also our acknowledgement of the limitations of rationalizing feeling. Of course, I did not tell this to her. What I did say, however, was that I thought she associated beauty - more than anything else - with tranquillity. White and aqua and teal, all had that quality in common.

S thought the game was over and lay back again, turning on her side and hugging me, as she is wont to while going to sleep. As she lay quiet, her eyes droopy but not yet closed, I asked her one last question.

"What colour is nostalgia?"

"What is nostalgia?"

"Looking back to the past… with longing"

"Longing…?"

"Missing…"

"Oh, like missing Amsterdam?" She was referring to the first five years of her life in Amsterdam, when she lived with both her parents.

"Yes", I said, returning her wistful smile with mine.

"It's grey and white, Mamma… memory is grey and white".

She had transitioned from 'missing' to 'memory' seamlessly. I did not point that out to her, nor to the fact that she named 'white' as the colour of both 'beauty' and 'memory'. I was not sure whether what she said about colours was long thought-out associations in her mind or just spontaneous responses in a conversation. But that the Kandinsky video and her art assignment played a part in it, I had no doubt.

We went to sleep that night dreaming of colours.

Brief previous association

S has two-night duties: setting the morning alarm on her phone, and turning on 'peaceful' music (a new fetish of hers) while she is already in bed and waiting for me. I invariably take more time than I intend to before joining her, which irritates her no end. During the weeks of her Kandinsky exercise, the default music became 'Moonlight Sonata'. I did not mind. Listening to it one night, I told her of the woman Beethoven had composed it for, when his hearing impairment had already set in, and how he went completely deaf later. She was in shock and disbelief ("how can you compose music if you can't hear it") and refused to hear more about it. This has been her natural survival strategy in the last 4+ years after relocating to Kolkata – firmly shutting out the painful/ unpleasant things she cannot take, and shifting her attention elsewhere instead. In this case, she wanted to know of my brief previous association with Beethoven and Kandinsky, something I had mentioned to her in passing while she was drawing one afternoon.

Both predated her birth, in the two cities – continents apart – that I have known as home.

CSM

For more than a year, somewhere between 2004 and 2006, the first Friday of every month held a peculiar excitement for me. On those evenings, I would go to the Calcutta School of Music to attend a western classical music class by the late Kishore Chatterji. I was not alone. I had a dear colleague-friend of mine for company. She had an important reason to attend those lectures: working on T.S. Eliot and Western classical music as she did, she thought the course would help her in her research. I had a different motivation; I went because of an interest that I had never really pursued. A radio program airing western classical music that I listened to sporadically on Sundays in my teens would often move me to tears. That memory had stayed with me… years later, I now wanted to belatedly explore that emotional effect.

The accent in the class was on listening. Kishore da wanted to attune our ears to the music he loved. He spoke very little. It was either to preface a piece of music, or else, after playing it, he seldom interrupted to make a point in between. 15 years later, I cannot recall any specific evening or lecture. I just recall the ritual it had become: the first Friday evening of the month ritual, akin to a Friday night film show, in terms of anticipation and excitement. And this show never disappointed: it was one hour of pure delight, immersed in music in a semi-dark hall, with a group of intent listeners forming a silent community. For most of that hour, my eyes would be closed. When Kishore da spoke, I scribbled sometimes in a small notebook.

That notebook sat snug in an inner flap of a leather handbag that one of my dearest cousins had gifted me on my wedding: a brown, sleek affair that I used only on those evenings. The notebook, too, was taken out only then. My 'interest' developed into a kind of nodding acquaintance, over that year, with some representative pieces by Vivaldi, Bach, Mozart, Beethoven, Debussy, Tchaikovsky (among the ones I can remember now) and many others. Thereafter, however, once the classes stopped, there was no movement forward… till S was made to dance to Vivaldi's 'Spring' in 2018, in her first-ever public performance with her ballet class in Kolkata. 'Four Seasons' is the only piece of Western classical music that I can say I know well, after hearing it night and day for several months. 'Moonlight Sonata' is becoming a close second, this time prompted not by S's dance but her artwork.

VGM

Unlike Beethoven, my first acquaintance with Kandinsky was not in Kolkata, but Amsterdam – at a wonderful Exhibition on 'Expressionism' in the Van Gogh Museum (in 2007/2008). I distinctly remember being drawn to the work of Egon Schiele and bringing home a poster. Also, remember taking copious notes, copying down entire texts from the museum walls, starting with the one on the almanac 'Der Blaue Reiter' that had taken its name from Kandinsky's 1903 painting.

The poster had hung on the wall of the living room, in the rented apartment in Amstelveen we had first lived in, in the Netherlands. I am not sure whether I have any photographs of it, though in my mind's eye, I can still see it clearly. I have lost that first notebook, too, the one I used to take on my museum visits in the first two years. There is abundant material on Schiele and 'Der Blaue Reiter' on the internet; everything is Google-able these days, after all. I do not need to fall back on a long-lost notebook and its scribbles to access information. But I wish I could leaf through it now… if only to re-visit what struck me the most then.

I had also written a longish piece on the Exhibition – not exactly with publication in mind, but just in an effort to understand what I had seen better.

We had a museum just round the corner from where we lived - CoBrA Museum of Modern Art - across the 'Binnenhof', above which our block of apartments was located. Amstelveen Binnenhof also happened to be a tram terminus, that of Tram Lijn 5, that took one to Amsterdam Centraal station. Somewhere in between, mid-way, about 20/25 minutes into the ride, one reached Museumplein, close to the centre of the city, with a vast green in the middle, flanked on the one side by Concertgebouw and on the other far side by Rijksmuseum, with the Stedelijk and Van Gogh Museums in between. Dam Square - the other tourist hotspot - came a few stops later, half encircled by the royal palace and the Nieuwe Kerk. One reached the Centraal station a couple of minutes after that.

I loved the ride from Amstelveen Binnenhof to Museumplein, loved to walk the stretch of the plein and visit the Exhibitions at VGM.

In 2006, when I was there for only a few months, I had already visited the major museums of the city, buying museum guides for myself and postcards and gifts for family and friends from the museum shops. But when I shifted base in 2007, I would frequent VGM much more. I cannot recall all that I have seen, but I did visit some fabulous Exhibitions – the one on 'Expressionism' being one of them. Another, on John Everett Millais, stands out – not just for the gorgeous catalogue that I triumphantly brought home, but also and especially for the poster of 'Ophelia' that graced our new/owned apartment for years. I have many photographs of *that*.

I continued buying museum memorabilia and gifts over the years during my visits, sometimes eating in the museum cafeteria, or else, in Café Cobra on the Museum Square outside. VGM had become a kind of 'thyek' for me, especially in the first two years. It lessened considerably in the next few; and almost stopped after S was born. I visited twice after her birth – the first time taking her in a pram to the inauguration of a new building; and in the summer of 2016, I took my bestie (herself an artist) when she came visiting. Van Gogh had been a cementing bond between us way back in the 1990s when I had gifted Irving Stone's *Lust for Life* on one of her birthdays. She turned to art definitively after reading that book and Vincent became a part of us ever since.

✦✦✦

S didn't know about Expressionism or the Exhibitions I visited before she was born, and she had no idea of tram routes in Amsterdam, but she was well aware of the fact that VGM has a special place in my heart, as indeed the city of Amsterdam. It was CSM that was a complete revelation for her, and she heard about it with the same rapt attention that she gives to all my family stories. She loves digging into my past, especially my childhood with my sister. Also, any and every story to do with Amsterdam – which, for her, was basically Buitenveldert (the residential district in Amsterdam Zuid, where we lived) and our apartment on the ninth floor of one of the tallest buildings there.

It is remarkable how much she remembers of her first five years in that apartment and that neighbourhood. Her memory, as she told me, is shaded white and grey. Mine is always sepia-tinted. On moonlit nights, on the balcony of my Kolkata home, we sometimes share our nostalgia – feeling the same feeling in different colours, with Beethoven in our ears.

COMING OUT SOLO (2022)

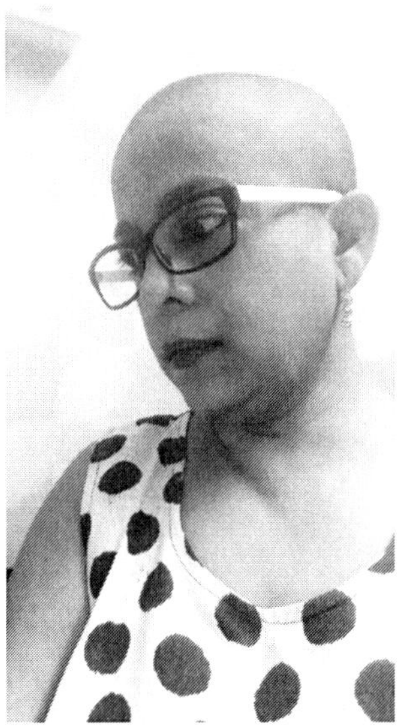

TWO YEARS of GJ (20 January 2022)

It has been two years now that *Gariahat Junction* was published!

This is an appreciation post. Also, one of the stock taking.

I would like to thank the same wonderful people I was grateful to two years ago (who were part of the publication process): Zafar Anjum and Kitaab International for publishing it; Arindam Dasgupta for the beautiful cover art and design; Kunal Basu, Saikat Majumdar and Sumana Roy for the generous blurbs.

The book's birth was greeted with enthusiasm: special thanks are due to Arunava Sinha for publishing an extract in Scroll; to Malavika R. Banerjee for making it part of a Panel at KLM-2020; to Koral Dasgupta for including it in a 'Writers-in-Conversation' online-series at TMYS (with Damyanti Biswas), during the first lockdown in 2020; to Tanuj Solanki for the very first, honest feedback on Goodreads; and three other gifted writers for their sensitive and nuanced reviews: Anurima Chanda (in The Punch Magazine), Dipika Mukherjee (in Jaggery) and Bhaswati Ghosh (in The Woman Inc.).

But I am most grateful to those who bought and read the book. A first-time fiction writer is a deeply insecure person and nothing encourages her more than when people buy her book to read. In my case, many were extra sweet and sent me photos when their copies arrived, and posted little notes about what they thought of the stories – on Facebook and WhatsApp (some of which I incorporated in short videos). They have found a permanent place in my heart!!

I am also thankful to those few - among the many I had gifted the book to - who got back to me with their feedback. I have to mention Prof. Sanjoy Mukhopadhyay here: on a quiet February afternoon in 2020, he called me and spent some 30 minutes telling me what he liked about the title story, going to some length talking about its 'cinematic quality'. I have not had a more flattering half-hour in the last 24 months!!

This appreciation post would be incomplete if I did not mention a few who have encouraged me as a writer, in their own different ways, in the last two years – Asijit Datta, Swaty Mitra, Swapna Bhattacharya, Gargyee Roy, Bhagwathi Rao Sandilya, Bratati Raybardhan, Brototi Das Gupta, Srinka Bose, Pinaki De, Debasish Mukherjee, Piu Mahapatra, Runa Chatterjee and Sudeshna Chakraborti.

Last year, I lost a reader - my father - to dementia, and found a new one in my daughter. My best and most devoted reader left me five years ago – I miss her every time I write; I cry every time I mention this. Her elder daughter - Nilanjana Ray - stands in for her, steadfast, to support me in all that I do and what I choose not to.

✦✦✦

I have not been able to write much in the last 24 months; or rather, not been able to write what I planned to – I have written X number of blog posts, Y number of essays, Z number of articles and reviews, totalling to so many thousand words; but a shelved novel remains shelved, a work-in-progress memoir does not seem to progress.

The problem is not always a question of time. Fact is, I have been wracked by an overwhelming sense of futility. Whatever I think of writing seems somehow irrelevant and meaningless in the face of what we are facing globally since 2020 – the relentless dance of death and disease, of unbearable pain and suffering, the maddening uncertainty of the times.

I am simply not able to handle writing a 'book', to give it the sustained attention it deserves; can only manage shorter pieces, and sometimes, nothing at all.

So much of what we 'do' is intangible work, I have realized. It cannot be put in a CV or posted on a wall; no certificate or photograph can encapsulate it.

My chief 'doing' of the last two years has been a profound questioning of and renewed confrontation with the self, both the personal and professional self. I have learnt new things about being a daughter and a mother; come to terms with the kind of work I really want to do; and realized what I will not, even under duress.

Most importantly, I have learnt - in a whole new way - the depth of my insignificance. It inspires me to pursue a project where I can think beyond myself. But it stands in the way of my writing…

✦✦✦

PS:

I have had to be my own chief publicist and PR agent, with GJ; I haven't enjoyed that at all. I have done it reluctantly, fitfully, incompetently – not posting anything for months on end in the first year, and almost forgetting the book myself in the second. I am not up to the relentlessness of the exercise… and I am not supposed to, either; my chief function as a writer is to write, after all.

But I did enjoy the process of creating a promotional video for it: I was both inside the book and outside of it while conceptualizing it; and I loved the fact that so much of my past and present came together in it, as also many dear ones.

In the long run, it is quite likely that this video will be seen more than the book read.

BACK TO SCHOOL (7 April 2022)

"Your school is finally re-opening, beta"!

There was a squeal of delight in response.

"And the good thing is that it will be just two days a week, initially – Monday and Thur..."

I could not complete.

"But whhhyyyyy"?

"Because it will be difficult for you to do a full-fledged school after two whole years of online classes, you know".

"Whhhyyyyy"?

She was talking like George now, Peppa Pig's little brother, whose "whhyyy's" could fill up entire episodes.

That was the story at the beginning of March. But the twice-a-week physical school did not continue for long. Just three weeks after the warm-up, it was back to full school.

Just before that, however, in the second week after re-opening, S fell in the playground during PE and injured herself badly: both knees were hurt, so was the right elbow, but the worst injury was near the right eye. It was a close shave! It was so near the eye that applying ointment became an ordeal, as it always threatened to touch the eyelashes and clamp them together. She had developed a secondary infection within a day of the injury, but thankfully, a five-day course of medicine and rest helped heal. And I was more than relieved when she was able to do the first full week of school from 28th March.

It is amazing how quickly one can get back to a routine, even after a gap of 24 months. I say 24 months and not two years, because those two were stretched out too long - for every one - and the slow unfolding of uncertain months had to be counted.

I had sorely missed our morning ritual of beginning the day together by dropping her off at school. Online classes gave us more time in the mornings, no doubt, but our 20 minutes of morning quiet in the car has been sacred to us ever since August 2017 – being the one stable point amidst several tumultuous years with changing schedules for me - and I am so grateful to get it back. We have also never been happier on Monday mornings...!

S's school is meticulous about all things academic and it continued to be so all through the pandemic, managing everything with superb efficiency through the LMS online platform. The teachers also worked very hard to give students the maximum they could within the limitations of the online mode.

Some schools had maintained reduced hours for online teaching/ learning during the pandemic, and many of us parents preferred that. At least, initially. I remember two consecutive academic years (in June 2020 and June 2021) began with lengthy discussions between parents and teachers/ administrators on this topic during Orientation Day.

Most parents basically wanted less screen time for their children. But it was rightly pointed out that if they did not have classes, they still spent time on the screen – on the phone, tab, laptop, or

TV. In our home, the TV is hardly on and we do not have a tab. But the phone and laptop are in overdrive. I had to buy both a new laptop and phone in 2020, and S, too, had to be given both, because after the first few months it was simply not possible to share the devices.

Her phone has now been confiscated, but the laptop has become a way of life that cannot be wished away. But at least, it will be resorted to only after school hours!

The joy of physical school for the kids is difficult to convey in words. It's best measure for me is the perpetual smile on S's lips at all hours of the day and night, the greater frequency of her laughter, and the sheer zest with which she starts off her day.

There is also another tiny little happiness tucked in her school bag that adds to the fun of school for her. The second flap of the bag carries her tiffin box. It has two small boxes within the bigger box: one contains something a little sweet; the other something a little salty. One of the great delights of her day is to open and see what goodies await her there. She consumes one, she tells me, during the first longer break (20 minutes) in the morning, and the other during the second shorter one (10 minutes) in the afternoon. The main food item seems almost irrelevant.

I just hope the months to come remain sweet and salty for her – adding zing to her renewed school routine!

TO STAND FIRM ON SLIPPERY GROUND
(8 May 2022)

In the last ten months, I had to shift my father to a dementia care facility, left my job, and got divorced after several years of separation. The pandemic played a part in these decisions and changed my life irrevocably. Of the three, the first has been the most painful decision of my life – one that I am yet to come to terms with emotionally. When Baba left home, it was not just a parent but also a child that I had to let go.

This is not the first time that my life has entered a radically new phase, but never before have I been without any of the proverbial anchors of life – parents, partner, a stable income.

In 2017, I had gone through one of the most difficult transitions in my life, even more than the one I had faced a decade earlier. But I did not lack support. I will be eternally grateful to Baba for never having once asked me why I returned to him 18 years after marriage with a small child; to my sister, who stood by me through thick and thin; and a few friends with whom I could be unapologetically myself.

To start from scratch at 43 was not easy… but for the first few years, I at least had Baba - however frail - with me. But what I am facing now was unimaginable even a year back. I had honestly never thought I would come to this pass; that I would bring up a child in my home city with my own family nowhere in the picture – with Ma gone, Baba lost to a disease, and didi continents away. My family was not near me in my child's first five years as well – but that was in Amsterdam, not Kolkata.

In the last few years, it has been tough to retain my right to choice in both my personal and professional lives. But I did not, for a moment, stop believing that that right was mine. That is, in fact, the only legacy I want to bequeath to my daughter – never to give up on the right to choose. Not even when, but especially because, it is the hardest thing in the world: because all through a girl-woman's life, people will either refuse that right or try to snatch it away from her. And those 'people' include her dearest ones.

✦✦✦

The day of my divorce, I was looking for a single song/poem/image that could encompass the entire arc of a decades-long relationship... but could find none… probably because an ocean of memories cannot be distilled into any one configuration.

With regard to this new phase in my life, too, the search for myth and metaphor has been an abiding one.

The Greek myth of the phoenix rising from the ashes is frequently invoked to enable tales of women overcoming great challenges to find themselves. But it does not work for me. The phoenix stands, in different readings, for immortality and resurrection. And there is a certain grandeur about her rising from the ashes. Also, something definitive: of emerging into a glorious new being.

My experience has nothing grand about it. Its defining features have been contingency and precarity. And there is something still very malleable and undefined about my identity now, in terms of the work I do/ want to focus on doing. But that I am a mother has been rammed home into me during the pandemic in a way it was never before.

I have realized that, to be a mother – in the iteration that I am living out – is to stand firm on slippery ground. By a sheer act of will. And that will can never be forsaken, at any cost.

I have also realized, in a whole new way, both the crushing enormity and the infinite tenderness of living for one's child.

The widow of the dead soldier in Tennyson's famous poem, stunned with grief, finally cries when her child is placed on her lap by an old nurse. "Sweet my child, I live for thee", she sobs. But it is just not widows mourning the husbands they loved who are driven to this realization. Many mothers, in very different situations, also find themselves in the same spot.

✦✦✦

Some of those mothers battle all through their insignificant lives. No laurels await them, not even acknowledgements. They just need to keep getting better at the game of survival, hoping to thrive one day: a tall order as they age, as their body and mind start failing them. This piece is in solidarity with those insignificant lives that will remain insignificant forever.

'Mother's Day' is the day when social media erupts with beautiful photos and sweet memories by (seemingly) grateful children. The perspective can, however, be very different from the mothers' side.

FAREWELL FROM HOME (19 June 2022)

I thought I was having a heart attack. Had a terrible, terrible pain in my chest. Just could not get myself up from bed. Could not breathe for a while. Then had a panic attack when the pain refused to go… if I could not get out of bed, how would I take Baba? An ambulance was due in two hours. And Baba's paid caregiver (the fifth in eight months) was about to leave in three days, after having first threatened to leave without notice. Everything had to be arranged at gunpoint. There was no room for error. Not even by a hair's breadth.

The ambulance came, but not the one I had booked. There was no AC. It did have the machine, but apparently it had become dysfunctional that morning itself. And the ambulance, for some strange reason, could not find the right road. So, I was giving directions over the phone for over half an hour, and then I had to go down and walk out of the building, to find it two streets away and bring it, like a truant boy. I have never done that before – walk out to find a vehicle and bring it home; our address is pretty easy to locate in our neighbourhood. It was so absurd: at one point, in that half an hour, I was wondering whether the ambulance would reach the right street. Will reach me at all.

It was early July 2021, the peak of the second wave of Covid and emergency services were not easily available. The uncertainty in that little window of wait again made my chest pain flare up, after having allowed me to just about do the needful that morning.

After the ambulance arrived, taking Baba down was a quick affair. Everything had been kept ready: his clothes, medicines, a few items of personal care and extra linen. Two pairs of seasoned, hardy hands briskly lifted him out of bed and into the stretcher. He looked frighteningly thin and small even in that narrow space. He did not want to wear his diaper, as usual, but I could somehow persuade him to. He looked lost, confused, and tried to hold on to my hand all the while.

The arrangement in the ambulance was not what I had thought it would be. The things were kept as such that I had to sit beside Baba, not facing him. If I had faced him, I could have easily seen the traffic (through the glass part of the door) just by turning to the left (the windows were curtained and shut); but I was sitting beside him, so I had to turn back. But every time I did, the pain in my chest would increase. Even otherwise, it was stubbornly there. I had to keep one hand on my heart throughout in a feeble attempt to stave off the pain. With the other, I held Baba's hand; sometimes, held his body, trying my best to absorb the jerks that rattled his frame and scared him.

I stayed like that, throughout the one-and-a-half-hour journey – somewhere between sitting and reclining, holding Baba, with a hand on my heart. It was that one extraordinary moment in my life when the literal and figurative merged.

I said 'one-and-a-half' hours... but that journey had seemed an eternity to me! And I was just hoping and praying that we would reach the facility safely. My greatest fear was… not just Baba reaching well, without any kind of emergency on the road (which I frankly did not know how to deal with), but now, almost as much, that I would be able to reach that place in one piece! For 90 minutes, I was sincerely not sure of that.

✦✦✦

The last time Baba was in an ambulance was in 2018. An ambulance had then brought him back home: from a prolonged stay in hospital, after a near brush with death following a freak kidney failure. He had been confined at home ever since, and the last year, mostly confined to bed.

His general health deteriorated in 2020 and things went spiralling down all through that year; but it was in early 2021 that it began going out of control, after dementia set in and care giving, already precarious, became all the more challenging, as trained help was nearly impossible to find in Covid times. He was particularly unfortunate in having a string of unreliable caregivers who took no time in abusing their power over him and taking advantage of my vulnerability.

The last eight months of his life at home were a nightmare I do not wish to recount. A point came when I had to take recourse to what I was not even willing to think of, even a year back. It is didi who helped me see the reality of my situation and act accordingly.

✦✦✦

To institutionalize Baba in a dementia care facility has been the most traumatic decision of my entire life – in a way, even more than leaving my marriage after 18 years.

It has been traumatic principally for two reasons. The first is cultural conditioning: in our culture, we still cannot think of the elderly living anywhere else but their own homes (an issue that requires a wholly separate discussion, which I am not going into here). But it is the second reason that made it more painful for me: I had returned to Baba after a failed marriage. And he – old, frail, just widowed – had still, without the least hesitation, received me with open arms. I returned to him, to his home… and then had to shift him from that very home. That is an irony that was/still is very difficult to accept. And there is an attendant guilt to it that was/still is very difficult to overcome.

Guilt is directly proportional to gratitude. Baba has been a good father to both his daughters, but my gratefulness to him is of an altogether different order. In the last four years, it was very difficult to decide who depended on whom more – me on him, or he on me. But there can be no denying the fact that I took a very big decision in my life and I could not have carried it out without him.

✦✦✦

It has been almost a year now that Baba has left home.

I mourn his loss. I mourn his loss to a disease that is random, cruel and incurable. Worse: indefinite. To suffer from it, to deal with it, is to live in eternal limbo. There is a finality to death, which, however painful to the deceased's dear ones, allows them to recalibrate their lives in terms of an absence; and most importantly, is merciful to the patient. That mercy is not in human hands.

Baba is in good hands now, I know. That should suffice. But I really wish he did not have to go through this.

He has been such a generous man. All his life, he has only given to others – his time, energy, money, and advice. He should have been left with at least some dignity. But that was not to be.

He is/was a proud man: proud to live in a home he owned, on his pension; and till 82, upright, on his feet.

I wish that pride had not been taken away from him. I wish he could continue in the comfort of his own home, in the company of his family.

I miss him. I will always need him.

A MOMENT OF ETERNITY (30 Aug 2022)

I was inordinately late for the pickup that Friday afternoon. I had informed S's class teacher in the class WhatsApp group about my delay, but the text did not go through because of bad connectivity. And I got caught up in traffic on the road, the kind that only monsoons in Kolkata can throw up. When I reached, there was not a soul to be seen anywhere: no cars, no police, no children coming out of the gates with their parents or escorts, not even the trickle of late pick-ups. It felt eerie. For a moment, as I stepped out of the car, it felt like I had come to the wrong place.

I had not. It was just a familiar setting of five years rendered unfamiliar by the absence of predictable details. I would experience something else soon.

By the time I had reached, it had been pouring heavily for more than an hour. And in the few seconds that it took me to open the door of the car, open up my umbrella and step out, the rain was already slashing hard against me, wetting my left arm and leg. I was wearing a pair of light cotton skirt and blouse that day, with a pair of slippers. The most casual of casual wears, which allowed a greater play of rain and wind on me.

In pre-pandemic times, on rainy days like this, cars are allowed in to take the children. They circle round a tree, in front of the portico, as they move in and out of the school premises, in a torturous long line. This orchestrated movement of vehicles coincides with the shrill of children delighting in the rain, in a heady mix of control and abandon.

Post-pandemic, once the school reopened, parents have not been allowed inside the main school building; and in the few months of school till the monsoons, there has never been the kind of rain that necessitated cars going in to pick up the kids.

I (wrongly) assumed that day that the car would not be allowed; hence walked in, rain-slashed, wind-blown – beneath an umbrella that dripped its own water, in eight parallel lines encircling me. I have always marvelled at that geometry!

✦✦✦

S was waiting for me. But her impatience for my arrival had already worn thin by the time I did, and she had settled into chatting with one of her attendant 'didi's. Her lips broadened into the widest smile seeing me wet. Didi asked us to wait out a bit. We did; watching the rain bathe both the concrete and the green of the school, listening to its peculiar music. I had a strange feeling of déjàvu, as I stood there.

The rain showed no signs of abating. Fearing it would get worse, we walked to the car.

It must have taken us seven/eight minutes to walk from the portico, down the straight tiled path to the school gate, and out to our car. It takes much less than that on normal days. S and I were slowed down by the rain, and the fact that we were sharing an umbrella to shield ourselves from it. We did not mind the slower pace; we could have even embraced slow-motion. The eight parallel lines of rain dripping from the umbrella were now encircling us both. It was the most beautiful circle of joy that we have known. Both of us (two giggly girls now, not mother and daughter) wanted to throw it off and surrender ourselves to the rain. Only the fear of falling sick again (S had just recovered from Covid a few weeks back and we both catch cold easily) stopped us. Still, we got drenched – S, half; me, almost full.

✦✦✦

The day after, I showed S a short video. Told her it was from August 2017; her first day of school after relocating from Amsterdam to Kolkata. We had stood at the same spot, waiting out the rain (though the car had come in that day). "But Mamma, it looks like you have taken the video from yesterday", she said. I agreed.

It did look like it. In fact, it was. The same moment, resuscitated over time. Over half a decade.

She was five then; she is ten now. Our lives have undergone enormous changes in between. We are no longer what we were in 2017. Yet, this moment has remained just the same: only enjoyed by a taller S and a greyer-haired me.

Sometimes I feel our lives are nothing but an endless resuscitation of earlier moments: earlier moments from our own lives, and those of our parents/grandparents/ancestors (however different the external trappings may seem). Through the unfailing rhythm of the seasons. And it is through these moments that we partake of eternity. As against immortality.

We desire immortality; we wish to continue in our children and loved ones; we pour our energy into doing things that we hope will last forever... but in reality, we are just specks in time, whirling temporarily through the immensity of space.

Tiny moments of eternity connect us to those who have been here and gone before us, and to those who will come after.

✦✦✦

This month has been a roller-coaster of an altogether new kind in my life. All through the crests and troughs, I held on to the memory of that rain-washed moment several weeks ago. To its beauty and innocence. And the unalloyed joy it gave us, however briefly.

I also reminded myself, I am just a tiny speck in time...

ধিক! ধিক! ধিক! (I CONDEMN!) – 5 Sept 2022

Of applications and interviews, while starting over:

Spring 2017. I flew down from Amsterdam to give an interview. It cost a fortune. But the stakes were high. We were relocating back home to Kolkata after a decade abroad and I was having to start over from scratch. A University job, even if at the lowest rung, would help me find a foothold. Or so I thought.

The interview was a sham: I was not allowed to go through even half my Demo lecture, was quizzed on Medieval English literature like a KBC rapid-fire, asked a few more perfunctory questions, made to hear condescending remarks, and dismissed. By then, of course, it had been established that I know nothing!

To this day, I have not been able to understand why I was called for that interview, when the University requirement was for a Middle-English expert (which is what I came to know later). Did they not read my CV? Did they not see my specialization was Indian English literature and that I had worked on Partition fiction in both my Ph.D and Postdoc, with two books on the subject? More importantly, did they not know I was bearing this huge personal expense (an international ticket on very short notice) to try and get this job? I had contacted the office several times from Amsterdam in the course of couriering my application. What kind of sadism was this? Staged interviews are not new in our educational system in India. But why make a candidate lose so much money?

I had not come for my Convocation in 2008, because it was within a month of our annual visit that year. I did not want that expense to be incurred twice in such a short span. Hence, I had taken a provisional certificate with me. The memory of that haunted me in 2017.

The memory of that first interview, in the wake of my relocation to Kolkata, would also haunt me since: the dashed hope, the loss of money. The humiliation during the interview by a distinguished professor whom I had long admired as a scholar.

In another interview - this one was after relocation - I was selected for an interview and then asked not to come. As the recruitment authorities could not decide on my API score, and hence on the designation that I had applied for.

In a third, there was no panel for the interview. The well-known professor of a reputed university who was supposed to take my interview said she had never, in her decades-long career, been part of a one-person panel! She was the panel, as it happened, and we ended up chatting about my life and career. I respected her for being candid about the hoax of the interview, while still engaging with my teaching and research experience. Nobody, anywhere else, before or after, seemed to be interested in that.

In a fourth, I went through three rounds of interviews after the Demo lecture, with successive levels of management, spread over a month, bargaining about the salary like buying fish in the market. I was the fish here. They were trying to fix my price.

For the first year after my relocation, I was a guest faculty at a hallowed institution, in which I would have liked to continue in a full-time capacity. But there were no vacancies there in the general category for which I could apply. One did come up and was advertised at one point, but nothing came of it… no recruitment followed from there, of anyone. And the department itself seemed to have no clue about the matter.

There were a few others – long, tedious applications all. In some, I applied very early; in others, I was late. Most of them were desperate, yet reluctant applications – driven by sheer need. I wanted the jobs and dreaded having them at the same time!

This was my interview/application experience from early 2017 to late 2019 – in universities and private institutions in Kolkata (most of them new). I had to restrict myself to these two categories for two reasons:

- I was well past the age for College Service Commission and hence had to rule that out. I had, in fact, started my career in 2001 through a full-time CSC posting (in a South Kolkata college) and had become 'permanent' a year later – but I had left the service in 2007. That door was now closed for me. And in any case, I could not have taken any posting in West Bengal outside of Kolkata, which would have most likely been the case with CSC.

- I could not apply outside of West Bengal, for personal limitations (though the temptation to do so was high).

My career options were thus limited. In one's mid-40s, with a child and other familial responsibilities, that is usually the case. Especially for women.

Stability and respect

This post is not about the challenges of starting over in one's 40s with a small child. That was a personal choice that had been dictated by unfortunate circumstances. And that journey would have been difficult, anyway, even if I had been in some other profession.

It is also not about particular institutions, which is why I have refrained from naming them. In my understanding, they are all part of the same vicious system, and the differences between them are really one of degree, not kind.

In four years, I taught at four institutions – as a Guest faculty in two in the first year (these were among the oldest institutions in the city, where I taught for the length of my contract); and as full-time faculty in another two over the next three years. In the latter, I taught in one for a little over a semester, and in another for two years. In both the full-time jobs, I had entered with the hope of continuing, in fact, of building a career afresh. God knows, I needed some stability in my life. A stable job was important for that. But I had to leave both.

The most ironic part of my leaving was that I had had good working relations with both colleagues and non-teaching staff in the institutions I resigned from, not to speak of bonding with students. And there had been no direct confrontation with any authority, either. If anything, I had been treated with respect by them – in outward forms of address and manner, that is. But the only respect that really counts in a professional sphere is when one is given one's due, in terms of designation and salary, and one's contribution is valued. Respect also has no meaning in a fiercely exploitative environment.

Devaluing of teachers

Getting recruited was one thing, teaching quite another. There were absurdities I experienced I would not have imagined possible: an entire department being run with only two full-time faculty (one of them in an ad hoc position) and two guests, roped in later; a Bachelor's and Master's course begun simultaneously, in the maiden semester of a university. And, as if that was not enough, plans of RET being conducted, underway, in the second semester. Another thing I will never forget is having to take CL during Christmas week!

Things may have changed later, but I faced the worst of it in the initial months, being in charge of a fledgling department with scant resources. And I also suffered a health breakdown soon after.

Private institutions are a different universe, I was told; they are run on corporate principles and timings, but without the salary and other perks of a corporate job. One is hard put to accept that. It is harder, still, to gulp the fact that institutions can be run with no uniform recruitment or promotion policy; worse, with no vision for the future of either individual departments or the institution as a whole. Just a workable functionality being aimed at year after year... till the next impending NAAC visit rouses everyone into suddenly remembering and hastily following UGC guidelines.

The worst thing, however, is the devaluing of teachers as utterly disposable commodities to be bought at the lowest possible price.

This ultimately has to do with a botched supply and demand ratio. The supply of qualified unemployed young people, at any point, is at least ten times more than the demand for any vacancy in any institution, making it possible for private employers to recruit early-career academics (with little or no teaching experience) endlessly. They join to gain experience before their CSC/PSC posting happens, or out of fear that it might not happen, or happen in a location they cannot accept. They continue where they begin, as CFTs mostly, and the way up from there is always uncertain.

These are people who have invested years of hard work in trying to enter this profession -- with excellent grades, NET/SLET qualification, and some research experience (they are usually young scholars who have just finished their M.Phil./Ph.D.'s or are working on it). And many are here because they genuinely love to teach. But that love soon turns into disillusionment when they don't get the salary they deserve, or are supposed to (which can be anywhere between half and one-third the regular scale). And they also find soon enough that there is very little opportunity for growth as a scholar, which the profession demands, but their long teaching hours and administrative/other responsibilities on campus don't allow.

When they do leave for their CSC/PSC jobs, or better opportunities outside the state (sometimes reluctantly, after years of service to an institution), they are replaced easily by those in line. No effort is made to retain even the best and brightest of them. And so, it continues. With departments becoming merely transit points in uncertain career paths, rather than a dedicated site for the dissemination of knowledge of a particular discipline.

That dissemination does happen, but not in the structured way it should. It is random and utterly contingent, with new teachers constantly coming and going – disrupting the teaching-learning rhythm of the department, as well as teacher-student relationships, which is ultimately inimical for both.

I Condemn!

All this is so shameful! I condemn what goes on in the name of higher education in many institutions. As I said before, they are all part of a vicious system: one where educational excellence, nay education itself, is the last priority for those in control. And where – for all the corporate talk – the only investment that is not done is in the educators.

What I have faced in the last few years has been experienced by countless others, many of whom I know personally.

I am a middle-aged woman now, and have been a bit of an anomaly in the system I tried to re-enter. But my heart breaks when I see young people losing faith in this profession, owing to what they are experiencing very early on in their careers. I cannot blame them. I only hope things will change... and soon!

CREATURE OF THE SUN (10 September 2022)

As someone who has battled depression for a long time, I stand in solidarity with all those who suffer from any kind of mental illness – inherited or otherwise.

It is important to think of it medically and treat it like one would any other illness/disease. With the same kind of objectivity. It is important not to dismiss it, but also to normalize it – this may seem contrary, but it's not.

Professional help is a must. Yes, it needs time, opportunity and money. But so does any other treatment. Family and friends may give a listening ear, if one is lucky, but only a professional will know exactly what one needs and how much. Exactly where one stands with the illness. One can then work one's way out from there - slowly, painfully.

The biggest difficulty in suffering mental illness is not so much the illness itself as trying to overcome the fear of (oneself and one's family) being judged and stigmatized if one expresses it, and the guilt of spending money to heal it. I know this from experience.

✦✦✦

I am essentially a creature of the sun and I am determined to find my light... though it does seem impossible at times.

A big hug to the multitudes out there - some of whom I know - who are journeying through the same darkness.

SHUBHO BIJOYA (5 October 2022)

Looking back to Dashami 2012. Voorschoten, the Netherlands.

It was the only time that I 'performed' the "eiyo stree" (the married woman) to perfection – wearing every item that stamped my status: from sindur, sakha-pala and mangalsutra (this, a nod to the Bihari bahu I was) to donning the saree sadharan-style.

It was the third year of our full-blown, four-day Bengali Association Durga Pujo in NL and the first for us as parents. Our baby was only five months old then, and we were still trying to get used to the vast change in our lives, thirteen years after marriage. She was most definitely a bundle of joy, who gave us hope... that henceforth, things would be better – for us, between us.

With her in our midst, that Pujo was very special. And Dashami was somehow extra gregarious. We, at KALLOL, had developed a ritual for this day: apart from the customary 'sindur-khela', couples (some 20 of them) would pose for photographs, in as much of PDA as they could muster.

We had very few photographs together. And in all our 4+13 years as a couple till then, my husband would pose in only one way -- with an arm held gingerly around my shoulder, looking into the camera with a smile (which, depending on who was behind it, would range from formal and friendly to spontaneous).

He did the same this time, too, but something more intimate was demanded. I tried negotiating a middle ground... but then we both gave in... holding each other close: heads touching, shoulder and waist encircled, palms clasped.

Four photos mark this progression; each, unfortunately, a low-resolution one, with the last – and sweetest one – the blurriest of them all. I bemoaned this fact for many years... but now find it symbolic.

✦✦✦

Of all the festive occasions of the year, Pujo has been the toughest for me to reinvent in the past five years, as it has overpowering familial and marital associations.

Festive occasions are never moments of unalloyed joy, though they are supposed to be that. For many, in fact, the relentless 'fun' of almost a week-long Pujo can be both difficult and tiring to deal with – because of the prolonged effort it requires to keep up and mesh in with the joy of others, when they are not feeling it within themselves. Joy cannot always be drummed up with the beat of the *dhak*.

And yet, life goes on… and we learn new ways of living.

✦✦✦

শুভ বজিয়া, friends! May the goddess give us all the strength to fight our battles and slay the demons, both within us and in society at large.

May she also give us the resources to create our own happiness and prosperity.

PUJO HAIRCUT (12 and 13 October 2022)

I shaved off my hair completely in October 2020, just before Pujo that month. About a fortnight later, while posting a selfie of mine with the shaved head on social media, I captioned it 'Pujo hair-cut'. But it was actually not.

It was an act fuelled by curiosity and convenience, but it was also an act of rage and mourning. The first pair of reasons is easier to deal with.

Not greying gracefully

I started greying from my early 30s. By the time my daughter was born in my late 30s, the grey had increased substantially inside and begun to show on the temples. I resisted colouring for a couple of more years and started at age 40. Not because of the supposed milestone, but because there was too much grey near the temples, which I did not like at all. And I kind of agreed (then) with my bestie that, since my face did not age much, the grey did not sit well on it. There was a kind of disparity there. I look younger than my age, I have always been told. In my 30s, people habitually thought I was at least a decade younger, which never failed to amuse/surprise me, as I had been through a lot since my late 20s/early 30s, and often felt old and tired within. The mental exhaustion would only increase right through my 40s.

I initially started colouring twice a year. For Pujo and my birthday, which are roughly five months apart. The very first time had to do with me anchoring a Pujo event of the Bengali Association in the

Netherlands. But hair grew fast, and the grey at the roots showed up soon after colouring, leading to irritation and frustration.

I usually went for a trim or a haircut with the colouring and I invariably felt light and happy on those days. But then the grey would be back in no time!

Appointments at the salon were another problem. They could not be frequent. I also found them expensive. Add to that the fact that the time and scope to visit the salon were always limited. Whenever it happened, it was invariably hurried – to be just got over and done with as quickly as possible, with always some reason or the other to rush back home. This was the case not only in Amsterdam - where I stayed for three more years after I started colouring - but also, more so, in Kolkata.

The appointment had to be taken for at least a few hours. I have never had the patience for beauty treatments (went for facials rarely and to pluck my brows only when they started resembling a bush); hair colour tested it to the limits, really. It had a prolonged process: shampooing, cutting/trimming, colouring (applying the colour and letting it absorb, this being the most laborious part), washing off, blow-drying and styling. Uff! Just listing this makes me yawn!

There were the other alternatives, of course: colouring at home or resorting to mehndi. I have never had the patience or energy for the former and I did not like the reddish tinge of the latter (though I knew it was the healthier option and had tried it once or twice in my annual visits to India).

I also increasingly did not like the way I looked with hair colour. Something was lost. The face did not look the same.

I was thus in a quandary: I did not like the (by now) shocking grey at the roots; I also did not like coloured hair.

I wanted to grey naturally. One could wait it out, allow the existing colour to wear off completely. But I knew that the process would be long and it would still be incomplete.

I was curious to see just how much I had greyed right from the scalp; I wanted to start over from scratch. But was unable to do it for a long while...

It is the pandemic that gave me the required push to start over. In multiple ways.

To begin with, in the first six months of lockdown in 2020, I was so completely exhausted and overwhelmed with work all the time, on all fronts – singlehandedly taking over all domestic chores at home, teaching online full-time, supervising my daughter's online classes and routine, looking after my very old and fragile father whose health deteriorated drastically, as well as working for KPM – that I was left with absolutely no time for even the most rudimentary aspects of personal grooming. A quick bath and an even quicker gathering of the hair into a severe bun was all I could manage. Oiling and shampooing, even once a week, became such a difficult task!

Getting rid of the hair, I reduced one work of the day for myself. The purpose was not to remain bald, but to have as little of it as possible, henceforth.

Compliments and censure

I posted a selfie of my shaved head a fortnight after I had taken it. I had done so immediately after leaving the salon, in the trial room of a clothing brand, while trying on a new maxi-dress.

I was taken aback by the response on Facebook.

I was surprised by two things: (1) Many complimented me; there were flattering comparisons to Sinead O'Connor, references to Parsis Khambatta. (2) The number of women who wrote that they had contemplated shaving off at some point, but did not dare to do so, or put it off indefinitely. This was the more surprising part.

There was some censure, of course; I had expected that! Also, concern was expressed by some close friends, who texted or called me separately, to know if I was alright.

I told my friends I wanted to grey naturally. That was the truth. But not the whole of it.

✦✦✦

The whole truth

I had hesitated to shave off my hair for one more reason than the ones I enumerated before.

For the longest time, a Hindu married woman with a shaved head meant only one thing – a widow. It is the worst fate that could befall a woman. While the loss of a husband is a loss in any culture at any time for any woman, for a Hindu woman, it had meant a particularly virulent form of destitution, where she was relegated to the margins of society – stigmatized lifelong by a bewildering array of exclusionary social rituals and practices, practiced daily or during family celebrations or community festivals. Her options were either to remain somewhat of a domestic help in the extended family, often being predated upon by the men at her in-laws, or worse, being banished to Kashi (Benaras) – forced to live a life of denial.

This image of the destitute widow - clad in all-white, with shaved head and sorrowful eyes - is so seared into our cultural imagination, bolstered by stories in literature and visualized in films, that it still overpowers the later 19th century narrative of widows, enabled by the life-affirming reforms of Vidyasagar, whereby she could not only re-marry, but more importantly, have a rudimentary education. The scope of that education only increased in the 20th century, and a later generation of widows could not only study but also earn and sustain their families. Of course, they could eke out only a precarious living, but it was definitely a far cry from the Kashi-bound widow of yore.

When I thought of shaving off my hair, what deterred me most was this association with widows – never mind that bald-headed widows hardly exist anymore! I knew that when people would see me thus, the first thought that would mistakenly come to their minds would be of a reality that was not mine. I did not want them to have that thought, even for a moment. Hence, I deferred.

However, the reality that was mine was getting hard to bear.

✦✦✦

After more than three years of separation, I was getting tired of being in that peculiar no-man's-land of being neither married nor divorced. I strongly felt the need for closure. A legal closure was important, not just because we had had a registry marriage in addition to a social/religious wedding ceremony, but also because it would give formality/finality to an arrangement we had already settled into for a fairly long time. This was, however, easier said than done.

I had sought informal legal advice from a college senior, a High Court advocate, during a particularly fraught period, much before the pandemic, and it was understood that she would represent me when I was ready for legal proceedings. But unfortunately, she died suddenly in 2020 from cancer. And I had neither the time nor the energy to look for a new lawyer. But I also could not continue in the liminal space I found myself in.

In 2017, I really wanted to start a new life in a new place – one which had no association with my previous life. But that option was not a very feasible one with a small child. Her easy transition to a new school in (what was for her) a wholly new environment was the first thing that had to be addressed (and of course, the admission process had to begin much before relocation). My life had to be arranged around her school routine and not the other way round. This is to state a given. But givens are never easy to deal with, however easy they may be to theorize, especially by those who do not have to face them.

Living in the same city as her father ensured that she had weekends with him, as well as part-vacations and other festivities without any hassles. There was also more room for being flexible and dealing with emergencies, this way. For the first five years of her life in Amsterdam, she had lived with only us. And she loved/loves her father. Our separation was already a huge blow in her little life… I did not have the heart to make it worse for her.

She missed her life in Amsterdam terribly, but she did not understand the 'blow' till much later.

✦✦✦

We relocated back to Kolkata in late July 2017 to start her new school. Her father returned six months later, after wrapping things up in Amsterdam. During the intervening period, we would have in any case lived at my natal home with my father, who had been recently widowed. He had lived entirely alone for a year; having us with him thus gave him great joy.

At 81, he was a pretty active and agile man, firm on his feet and still capable of weathering storms – as I found out. He absorbed the shock of my separation with a stoicism that still amazes me. He would pick up S from school, make tea for me in the evening when I returned after teaching (I had taken a Guest position at the English Department of Presidency University, for the time being), potter around the house doing this and that, and instruct the house staff like a true mistress. But his health started deteriorating unaccountably just two months after my return, and after another two, he suffered a freak kidney failure and was hospitalized for almost five weeks, most of which was spent in the ICU. Didi happened to be here then; she managed the prolonged medical emergency almost single-handedly, even as she was recovering from a knee surgery herself, and after exhausting her extraordinary leave, went back to her work and life in the US.

In the long months at home after hospitalization, when Baba was first bedridden and then limped back to a fragile normality, there would have been no question of my living anywhere else but with him – even if I had not been separated. S understood this; that her Mamma needed to be with her Dadu to take care of him. That became the default mode of her existence. But somewhere, there was an uneasiness in her mind about this arrangement of her not being able to stay with her own father because her mother had to look after hers. It was not just that it was unfair, but there was something more to it that she could not quite fathom.

My heart broke every time I sensed that confusion in her, but I could not bring myself to tell her the whole truth. I could not continue living the half-truth of my existence as well.

✦✦✦

I felt caged. I had tried to break free of one but found myself in another. I was now stuck in Kolkata, for both my daughter and father, and doomed to exploitative work (with ignominious salary and designation) for as long as I could see. Worse: even my mobility within the city was restricted, given ayah/nanny timings and the vagaries of their attendance; forget travelling outside.

I felt rage, seething rage at what I perceived to be life's continual unfairness to me, which had started far back in time than my return to Kolkata in 2017.

I also felt rage because I was trying my best to be fair to those close to me, given the circumstances, but found it difficult, nay impossible, to be fair to all at once. Fairness, I discovered, cannot be balanced out equally: to be fair to oneself, one has to be almost invariably unfair to someone else; to be fair to a dear one would most likely necessitate being unfair to another.

But I felt rage most of all because I did not get the chance to mourn the death of my marriage.

✦✦✦

We mourn the death of a person through religious rituals, no matter which religion we belong to, or whether we believe in religion or not. Those rituals – whether spare or elaborate – are not just exercises in honour of the dead, but also an acknowledgement of a deep loss for the living.

Widows/widowers mourn the death of their spouses. But what about the death of a marriage, the death of a relationship? How does one mourn that? How does one mourn the long arc of deterioration from "I cannot live without you" to "I cannot live with you anymore"? How does one mourn the death of love, of connectedness in body and mind?

There must be as many different kinds of mourning as there are loves. But wives are not supposed to mourn when they are mothers, especially when they have themselves made the choice to break away. They are just supposed to get their act together and play the mother ever after.

In my case, there was just too much to deal with incessantly, one after the other, even apart from the child. There was no room left for mourning.

✦✦✦

I got rid of my hair in October 2020 – above all, for convenience at the time. But also, to register my rage and express my mourning to myself. There should be some outward manifestation of what I felt, I decided.

It was liberating!

EPILOGUE (2023–)

TIME'S WINGED CHARIOT HURRYING NEAR (May 2023)

> *"For at my back I always hear*
> *Time's winged chariot hurrying near*
> *And yonder before us lie*
> *Deserts of vast eternity".*

This reminder of mortality is the clinching argument of the lover, as he tries to persuade his coy mistress to shed her inhibitions and make the most of their youth and passion, in this famous 17th-century 'carpe diem' poem by the English metaphysical poet Andrew Marvell. It played no small part in the decisions of my youth!

I remember my legendary college professor Kajal Sengupta's tutorial on the poem. She had asked me, in the time-honoured CU tradition, to write a 'critical analysis'; and in her feedback on the next tutorial, launched into a long aside on "the nature of sexual passion" that I was totally unprepared for. It did, however, result in spiking my already latent curiosity about the subject!

The desire to "seize the day", enjoy the moment without thinking of the future, i.e., stemming from an acute awareness of the transitory nature of life – was thus, during college, primarily associated in my mind with sexual consummation at the earliest possible. After passing out, though, it somehow became "making the most of" other things. I tried hard to make the most of my 20s, with a whole list that I was determined to tick off before I turned 30: marrying the man I loved, a permanent job, Ph.D., and a baby. All I wanted was everything. And I had assumed that all of it would be in Kolkata. The first two in my list happened pretty early; the Ph.D. took almost three more years than my target years, but it is the baby that made a mockery of all lists. Almost another decade would pass by before she arrived, on another continent, changing my life - in the process of the wait - beyond measure, beyond imagining.

The baby and the girl

That baby is now 11 years old. I am faring a little better this year. I was shocked when she turned 10 last year. When did that happen?? She of dimpled cheeks and tiny curls and adorable lisp; who, till the other day, would jump up and down every now and then and say, "I am your bunny" (and look the part); who still has a habit of curling up in my lap like a cat (only the soft round ball of flesh has long limbs now). When did she grow up?? I did not realize that a decade had passed.

Time, that resource that I had wanted to make the most of in my 20s, and which became synonymous with 'waiting' in my 30s, had, in my 40s, become an adversary. An adversary I was constantly fighting and trying to get the better of. Days, weeks, months and years turned into just one long, relentless struggle with time; with clock time: to take charge of and integrate the routine of another life into mine; to accommodate ever more and new kinds of work; to acclimatize with frequent changes in schedules. And in my obsession with this clock time, a whole decade melted away.

Since I always lost to my adversary, the clock, there was also a sense of achievement (despite the shock) when my daughter attained the double digit. It meant she was now on the cusp of middle school. I felt the same kind of exhilaration I had felt when she first weaned, crawled, stood, walked, uttered her first words, went to pre-school, and kindergarten. Something concrete had happened, after all.

There are several barometers to mark a child's development, both in body and mind, in every phase of her growth curve. In primary school, its most obvious manifestation is the new subjects that get added to the curriculum every year. From Upper Nursery to Grade V, for S it has been Bengali, ICT, Drama, Social Studies, History, Geography, Value Education, and Foreign Language. In Grade VI, Science will be split into Physics, Chemistry and Biology. I have seen S's excitement with every new subject addition at every grade, and feel grateful that she enjoys school the way she does. But what I most cherish about her is her innate joy and her emotional maturity.

S is mature beyond her years. For more than half of her little life, she has already had to deal with a lot. I am not sure whether her maturity was born of it, going through it, or whether it is an innate quality that helped her cope with her circumstances. I just know that I could not have dealt with my altered reality the way I did, had she been any different.

Two of her primary school years coincided with the pandemic, which slowed lives down in unthinkable ways, but also speeded things up. Children grew faster, their brush with disease and death (whether direct or indirect) and the confronting of prolonged uncertainty, qualifying – to quite an extent – the innocence and joy of their childhood. If you added puberty to that picture, then a child was well on the road to experience.

A child's puberty is always hard-hitting for the parent, no matter how much one has prepared oneself, or the child, for it. Running tandem with that is the need for counselling, which I must say her school has done a wonderful job of, doing intensive counselling sessions with boys and girls separately. I remember the day S told me that she now knew about 's-e-x'. She spelled out the letters, as if I would not understand the word otherwise. They were also taught the reproductive system in science around the same time. I felt strangely sad the day she mentioned sex... for after this, I could not pretend she was small anymore. But I was also relieved that her endless curiosity about birth was finally satiated; for over the years, her questions had transitioned from "Mamma, how are babies born?" to "How long was I in your tummy" to (the most dreadful of them all) "How did I GERMINATE inside you"? (emphasis hers).

Growing through films

She is 11, but I can already see her as an adult. The incipient lady peeps through quite strongly when she wears Indian clothes during festivals – salwar-kameez, kurti, sarees (a Sarawati Puja special) – and I accessorize her in light jewellery and a bindi. With that, and her hair either tied up in a small bun or left loose and hanging, she transforms into this little woman!

She also responds like a little woman when we watch films together. We love going to the theatre, but during the pandemic, we watched a lot on OTT – in English, Hindi and Bengali, and a wide range in all. She is an attentive viewer; watches with great absorption, goes back to scenes she likes, and is full of questions (which can be very irritating at times). This side of her bloomed last year with her encounter with a number of literary classics on screen. The first was *Little Women* (we saw both the 1994 and 2019 versions). She liked all the March girls – Meg, Jo, Amy and Beth – and their friendship with Laurie, but it is the intensity of Jo's passion for writing and the lengths she was willing to go to for it that made the greatest impression upon her. (Also, I think, Amy's gowns in Paris)! It must be said that we both liked Greta Gerwig's film more, not least because of Saoirse Ronan.

We also watched a number of adaptations of Jane Austen on Netflix – *Pride & Prejudice* (2005, with Keira Knightley as Lizzy), *Sense & Sensibility* (1995, with Emma Thompson and Kate Winslet as the Dashwood sisters) and *Persuasion* (2022, with Dakota Johnson as Anne Elliot). We habitually watch a lot of films, but she loved these adaptations more than anything else I can remember; in particular, the female bonding at the heart of each (though their plots turn around love relationships). She made expert comments on the difference between the attitudes of the different mothers in dealing with the heartaches of their daughters. Though she admired Marmee March the most, followed by Mrs. Dashwood, its Mrs. Benett she found the most interesting, and laughed her head off in the scene where she accuses Elizabeth of being an "ungrateful daughter" (when she refuses to marry her cousin) – running after her along with a pack of wild geese, looking very much one herself, with her fluffy white gown on an ample frame.

Months after watching the film, S would suddenly remember that scene and erupt in laughter.

The other film where she had really enjoyed sibling bonding was Satyajit Ray's *Pather Panchali* (The Song of the Road, 1955). Which child will not respond to Apu and Durga? But that was four years back. And as a seven-year old, she had some very pertinent questions: "Did Durga really steal her friend's necklace"? "Why is the aunt SO old"? "Why is the mother ALWAYS angry"?

She watched a film on the making of the film last year (Anik Dutta's *Aparajito*), not long after the adaptations on Netflix. By then, she had completely forgotten the original by Ray, but enjoyed the recreated scenes, anyway! We revisited the classic a couple of months later, which she lapped up again!

Sarbajaya and me:

After watching 'Pather Panchali' with her, I re-watched the two other parts of the Apu Trilogy – *Aparajito* (The Unvaquished, 1956) and *Apur Sansar* (The World of Apu, 1959) – alone, the same day. Something changed in me as a viewer then.

For the first time in my life, I saw the first two films from the perspective of Sarbajoya – the mother of two children and wife of a village priest who has to feed the family (including an old aunt whom she resents) and manage the household all through their slow descent into poverty (most of it, with her husband away). For the first time, I also realized that it is her relationship with Durga, her daughter (and not Apu), which is focused in the film, in a series of riveting scenes: her fury when her neighbour accuses Durga first, of stealing guava from their tree (which she defends guardedly), and then a necklace (which she simply cannot take and beats the girl mercilessly); her persuasiveness when she explains to Durga (while tying her hair) the importance of learning domestic skills for a girl her age; the desperation with which she tries to save the fever-stricken girl on a stormy night; the stone she turns into the next morning after the girl dies; and her breaking down in the last scene when her husband returns with the gift of a saree for Durga, the high notes of the sitar in the background score filling in for her keening.

In 'Aparajito', we find the couple and their son in Benaras – in better circumstances, the husband with a steady income as a priest in this most sacred of cities. But his sudden death necessitates Sarbajaya's taking up a job as a cook in a wealthy household. Though treated well by her kind employers, she sees her son being reduced to an odd-jobs boy and decides to return to Nischindipur, the village in East Bengal they had left all those years ago. He trains to be a priest, like his late father, but his heart is set on going to a regular school, which he eventually does, and where he shines as a student and is offered a scholarship to study in Calcutta. The widowed mother is reluctant to let go of her son, but then relents – their confrontation scene is archetypical of all such moments in households where flying the nest is not understood as an inevitability of life.

What follows is another inevitability – the son being drawn to the bigger world of the city; with his studies, night-shifts at a printing press, and budding friendships preoccupying him, leaving very little time and inclination for writing letters to his mother.

The mandatory visits home during vacations are also reluctant and late. The mother wastes away in loneliness (the occasional company of kind neighbours notwithstanding) and an illness that is never diagnosed. The last time she entreats him to come see her, he sends her money instead, joking to his friend that it will compensate for his absence. He never sees her again. "On a night sparkling with evanescent fireflies, her life leaves her".

Sarbajaya and I are mothers a century apart. And there are also other obvious differences in our circumstances beyond the times we live in – except for the fact that we live alone with a child. Nevertheless, the second part of Aparajito resonated with me powerfully. In her fate, I could see my future.

MUSINGS: 2024

14 February 2024

And then there is the 'self' – that entity that we are told has meaning only concerning another (socially sanctioned) 'special' one. But the fact is, it continues to exist... with or without love, with or without a partner. All flesh and marrow, skin and bone, spine and skull, and a beating heart left in the torso. It is endowed with the same five senses as others (who are coupled) that respond to the same four elements of Nature, the same four seasons, the social environment and fellow sentient beings. The perceived 'lack' in its existence maybe a result of both circumstance and choice, but that does not take away the validity of its presence in the world. And its relation to itself.

Romantic love is at worst an illusion, at best an episode in most people's lives. For many others, it is a luxury they cannot afford, though they may long for it – like diamonds on billboards.

And some are so broken inside from past betrayals and take so long to heal that the possibility of 'new love' becomes redundant for them.

Taken together, these people probably account for a sizeable portion (if not the majority) of human beings on earth. One realizes then why the disproportionate presence of love in poetry and song and story: they articulate a desire, not a reality.

Ultimately, the self – and the body it's clothed in – is one's longest, uninterrupted companion in life.

20 March 2024

"There's a place in you that you must keep inviolate. You must keep it pristine, clean so that nobody has the right to curse you or treat you badly. Nobody. No mother, father, no wife, no husband, nobody".

Maya Angelou said this in an interview with Oprah Winfrey, about the best advice she has given her son.

It was said principally in the context of abuse. But, "There's a place in you that you must keep inviolate… pristine…" may also be read as a space within that's the ultimate refuge from the onslaught of the world… and of life itself; a relentless onslaught that is played out in myriad forms in daily life. Finding oneself is also about finding that inviolate spot.

26 March 2024

"You must move on", they say. And indeed, all around me, I see others moving on: buying and settling in new homes, starting over in a new city, finding new partners. I admire that ability. And I sure as hell know what it is to "start over"… but it is never a clean slate… never a tabula rasa; instead, always a palimpsest.

I have started over, but I am not sure I have moved on… I am still reformulating a new identity; still continuing to be the chief custodian of my parents' past; still emptying out old homes/once-homes, or filling up the content of one in another; still hoping for things that don't happen.

I guess I don't know how to move on.

10 April 2024

A recent book I read brought home to me, with great perspicacity, something I have often thought about – the inequality of need in human relationships.

We fight for equal rights, opportunities, resources – the things that determine the quality of our life and living. But we are absolutely powerless when it comes to our innate desire for an equality of need in the bonds that give our life meaning, and define, to a great extent, our mental and emotional wellbeing. That cannot be fought for; no impartial judge will dispense justice by levelling up or levelling down one person's need for another. One can only hope for it.

Otherwise, there is hurt, resentment, misunderstanding, or the gradual wearing off of something precious.

1 July 2024

It has now been seven years since I left my marriage; three, of living alone with a child.

I have realized that no matter how unimaginable a situation may have seemed once, one eventually learns to inhabit it.

And no, it does not get easier. One may just get better at donning one's armour (the proverbial chink notwithstanding) and taking things in one's stride.

Meanwhile, there is beauty to be gleaned from everywhere.

26 July 2024

She loved watching the moon from her mum's balcony, the stars from her dad's terrace. Living mostly with her mum, she would sometimes catch her crying in bed; her dad uttered not a word. She loved them both. And very early on, she had decided she would not miss one while being with the other.

She never forgot the home that was theirs, though – long ago, in a distant land. Never forgot its beauty, perched high, as if to meet the sky; never forgot the surrounding trees and canals, or the ducks and birds she met walking to school and back.

"When will we return"? she would ask initially. "Do the ducks remember me"? she wondered, a few years later. Then the questions stopped. But every year, on her birthday, she unfailingly saw two precious albums of their time together with her mum.

LIST OF PREVIOUS PUBLICATIONS

Saikat Majumdar quoted an extract from 'When Home is Not Home' in his column in **Outlook** in September 2020. With permission from the author.

- 'Ma on my FB Wall, in August', 'Durga Puja in Kolkata', 'Home-Quarantine Through the Eyes of a Seven-year-old' and 'Corona + Amphan' were published in **Authors Electric** – a blogging platform by an authors' collective, where I contributed from mid-2019 to late-2021.
- 'The Mark on the Wall' was written in June 2020 and published in an anthology edited by Asijit Datta, ***Stones and Bones: Fossils from the Pandemic*** (Chapakhana: 2022).
- 'Winding Joy' was published online in the 2021 Monsoon Special of **The Woman.inc**.
- 'Kandinsky meets Beethoven' was published online by **Outlook** in February 2022.

These pieces have been reproduced in this memoir with kind permission from the respective editors – Debbie Bennett, Asijit Datta, Pooja Garg and Chinki Sinha. I thank them all for their generosity.